# Michael M. Dediu

--------------------------------

# World Projects

----------------------------------------------------------------------

## Moving from minor projects to great projects for the World

----------------------------------------------------------------------

**DERC Publishing House**

Nashua, New Hampshire, U. S. A.

Published and printed in the
United States of America
On the Great Seal of the United States are included:
E Pluribus Unum (Out of many, one)
Annuit Coeptis (He has approved of the undertakings)
Novus Ordo Seclorum (New order of the ages)

**Library of Congress Control Number:  2020919517**

Dediu, Michael M.


World Projects
Moving from minor projects to great projects for the World


ISBN-13: 978-1-950999-23-1


1-9573770061
07136D
26Q8ET7
1-4EBZ4D8

# Preface

Having a good Constitution of the World, obviously many really important large projects for the world can be implemented, thus moving from small and inefficient projects, to large and efficient projects for all people. These world projects will create a completely new and much better level of civilization on Earth.

There are thousands of great world projects – we give just over 70 examples, from Building a lasting peace and Improving telework for all, to Virus control and elimination, and Hurricane prevention.

From the great philosophers Socrates, Plato, Aristotle, Descartes, and Kant, to the present day, many people dreamed of having really big and useful projects – finally, now we will be able to implement them for the benefit of all people.

This book discusses these over 70 projects, giving some details, emphasizing that these projects and the new ideas from the Constitution of the World, will create the conditions for a peaceful, free and prosperous new country, Peaceful Terra.

The future begins to take shape in front of our eyes, and it is amazingly beautiful!

Michael M. Dediu, Ph. D.

Nashua, New Hampshire, U. S. A., 20 October 2020

USA, New York: On West 42$^{nd}$ Street at Fifth Avenue, looking at Chrysler building (back up, Walter P. Chrysler (1875-1940), 1930, 319 m, 77 floors, 111,000 m$^2$ floor area, 32 elevators, at Lexington Avenue), before it is Grand Hyatt New York Hotel (1919, 90 m), and before it is Grand Central Terminal (1871, 1903, 1913, 2000, built by Cornelius Vanderbilt (1794-1877, the 2$^{nd}$ richest American, after John D. Rockefeller (1839-1937)) and his 13 children, commuter railroad terminal, with a grand façade, at Park Avenue, 47 acres, 44 high-level platforms, 67 tracks on 2 levels).

# Table of Contents

Italy, Rome (753 BC, one of the oldest cities in Europe, called Roma Aeterna (The Eternal City) and Caput Mundi (Capital of the World)), from the Pincian Hill looking southwest: Piazza del Popolo (1822), with the Egyptian obelisk (36 m) of Sety I (1290–1279 BC) and Rameses II (1303, 1279–1213 BC) from Heliopolis, brought in 10 BC by Augustus (63 BC-14 AD) for Circus Maximus, in 1589 here. Basilica San Pietro (1506, 132 m, back).

## Project 1. Elimination of war

**Description:** The objective of this project is simply to eliminate war and any type of conflicts on Earth, making possible for all the people on Earth to live better, peacefully, free, healthy, and prosperous.

**Management**: All the leaders in the world, with the help of the United Nations.

**Start day:** 1 November 2020

**Completion day:** 1 November 2021

**Budget:** $200,000,000

**Results after implementation:** Saving millions of lives, much better standards of living for all,
saving over $1,920,000,000,000/year.

**Comments:** It is a matter of common sense – all people want peace, freedom, good health, harmony and prosperity. For all the projects in this book, the author can be a senior consultant, to make sure that the projects are done on time and within budget.

France, Lyon, Place de la Comédie, l'Opéra National de Lyon (1831, 1993). At the upper façade of the Opéra there are 8 statues out of the 9 Muses: Euterpe (music), Terpsichore (dance), Thalia (comedy), Erato (lyric poetry), Calliope (epic poetry), Polyhymnia (hymns), Melpomene (tragedy), Clio (history) and the missing Muse is Urania (astronomy). The Opéra maintains its own permanent orchestra, choir, ballet, technical, costume and scenery departments. Preparation for a production starts two years before the first night.

# Project 2. Building a lasting peace

**Description:** The objective of this project is to have a lasting peace, without any conflicts on Earth, making possible for all the people on Earth to live better, peacefully, free, healthy, and prosperous.

**Management**: All the leaders in the world, with the help of the United Nations.

**Start day:** 1 November 2020

**Completion day:** continuous

**Budget:** $10,000,000

**Results after implementation:** Saving lives, much better standards of living for all, establishing self-supporting institutions, which work for lasting peace;
saving over $1,920,000,000,000/year.

**Comments:** It is a matter of common sense – all people want peace, freedom, good health, harmony and prosperity.
It is not sufficient to just eliminate war - we need to build a very strong and long-lasting Peace, because without peace not much else can be done. People want a Peaceful Terra.

# Project 3. Manage 509 M km² of land and water

**Description:** The objective of this project is to properly manage all the planet for all people.

**Management**: All the leaders in the world, with the help of the United Nations.

**Start day:** 1 November 2020

**Completion day:** continuous work.

**Budget:** $2,000,000/year

**Results after implementation:** Establishing self-supporting institutions, which work for clean and beautiful Earth for all people. Saving over $23,000,000/year with less expenses for health care, better agriculture products, etc.

**Comments:** The people will always have priority, with a proper balance.

# Project 4. Reducing the number of rules to 2000

**Description:** The objective of this project is simply to eliminate the many superfluous rules, which create bureaucracy.

**Management**: All the leaders in the world, at all levels, with the help of the United Nations, and the people.

**Start day:** 1 November 2020

**Completion day:** 6 March 2022

**Budget:** $20,000,000

**Results after implementation:** Saving millions of hours of inutile work, much better standards of living for all,
saving over $1,000,000,000/year from less bureaucracy, more efficiency, healthier people, etc.

**Comments:** This will be a continuous effort by all people.

## Project 5. Divide the Earth in 10 friendly regions

**Description:** The objective of this project is to create the conditions for a good and efficient management of the country Peaceful Terra.

**Management**: All the leaders in the world, with the help of the United Nations, and local people.

**Start day:** 1 November 2020

**Completion day:** 6 June 2021

**Budget:** $248,000,000

**Results after implementation:** Saving millions of hours of administrative work, much better standards of living for all, saving over $2,300,000,000/year with much better administrative work.

**Comments:** All people will participate. For easier administration, Peaceful Terra will be only administratively divided in 10 simple and friendly regions of around 770 M people each, called R0, R1,..., R9, which will be delimited by meridians (or line of longitudes), with the assistance of the United Nations.

## Project 6. Prepare cities to become capitals

**Description:** The objective of this project is to begin work for the preparation of many cities, which will become capitals.

**Management**: All the leaders in the world, with the help of the United Nations, and the local authorities.

**Start day:** 1 November 2020

**Completion day:** 16 June 2021

**Budget:** $32,000,000

**Results after implementation:** Improving local conditions, much better standards of living for all,
saving over $278,000,000/year by using much cheaper places.

**Comments**: Capitals will be everywhere, because the current capitals tend to become huge bureaucracies, with lots of people trying to be there, without much usefulness. Peaceful Terra will have moving capitals, to benefit everybody.

Each region will have a pair of capitals plus an outside city, for better and more homogenous management (all will change every year; more details are in the book "World with One Country & its Ten Friendly Regions - Moving from 195 disagreeing countries, to 1 country with 10 collaborating regions"). For example, the first implementation will be:
R0 between meridians 0 and $15^0$ E, capitals: Bern (Switzerland), Libreville (Gabon), and Oxford (UK).
R1: $15^0$ E - $30^0$ E, Warsaw (Poland), Pretoria (South Africa) and Miami (FL, USA).
R2: $30^0$ E - $45^0$ E, Moscow (Russia), Cairo (Egypt), and Grenoble (France).
R3: $45^0$ E - $75^0$ E, Astana (Kazakhstan), Karachi (Pakistan), and Montpellier (France).

R4: $75^0$ E - $85^0$ E, New Delhi (India), Novosibirsk (Russia), and Magdeburg (Germany).

R5: $85^0$ E - $100^0$ E, Krasnoyarsk (Russia), Urumqi (China), and Avignon (France).

R6: $100^0$ E - $115^0$ E, Jakarta (Indonesia), Beijing (China), and Neuchâtel (Switzerland).

R7: $115^0$ E - $180^0$, Tokyo (Japan), Sydney (Australia), and Malmö (Sweden).

R8: $180^0$ - $70^0$ Washington (USA), Mexico City (Mexico), and Bellinzona (Switzerland).

R9: $70^0$ W – 0 Halifax (Canada), Brasilia (Brazil), and Biel (Switzerland).

There are many big differences between the populations of different regions, in the first implementation, and then between the populations of different sub-regions, but this is just the first implementation, which needs to be quickly put in place, and then, very easily, the delimitations will be moved a few kilometers east or west, to reach a balanced population.

Because all the people are in the same country, it is normal to modify a little its regions, for better administration, to make everybody happy.

It is well understood that there will be some difficulties in the beginning, like in all beginnings, but with calm, patience, perseverance and hard work, the things will improve fast, and all the people will enjoy a better life.

UK, Oxford, from the Logic Ln, looking north to the High St and the south gate of the Queen's College (1341, founded by Robert de Eglesfield (1295-1349, chaplain of the Queen consort) in honor of Queen consort Philippa of Hainault (1314-1369, wife of Edward III of England (1312-1377, Reign 1327-1377, burial Westminster Abbey, they had 13 children, and their great-grandfather was King Philip III of France (1245-1285, reign 1270-1285))), University College (1249, left).

# Project 7. Define the sub-regions and districts

**Description:** The objective of this project is to define the sub-regions and districts, for better administration of the help for people.

**Management**: All the region leaders in the world, with the help of the United Nations.

**Start day:** 1 December 2020

**Completion day:** 26 July 2021

**Budget:** $120,000,000

**Results after implementation:** Saving millions of hours of superfluous work, much better standards of living for all,
saving over $410,000,000/year with improved administration and better help for people.

**Comments:** Each of the 10 regions will be divided by meridians in 10 sub-regions S00,  , S99, each with about 77 M people.
　　　　Then each of the 100 sub-regions will be divided in 10 districts: D000, D001,  , D999, each with about 7.7 M people, and each of the districts will have their current small and big cities.
　　　　All these delimitations between regions, as well as between sub-regions, will be flexible: these will be just simple administrative delimitations, and all these delimitations between regions, as well as between sub-regions, will be flexible – they will be changed after each census (5 years), for maintaining a balanced number of people in all regions (around 770 M) and sub-regions (around 77 M).

# Project 8. Improving telework for all

**Description:** The objective of this project is to extend and improve telework for all.

**Management**: All the managers in the world.

**Start day:** 1 November 2020

**Completion day:** continuous

**Budget:** $12,000,000

**Results after implementation:** Saving millions of hours of travel and stress, much better standards of living for all,
saving over $920,000,000/year from travel expenses, accidents, medical issues, etc.

**Comments:** This is the future – with telework many people will have a northern residence and a southern residence, seasonally moving from one to the other, to avoid extreme cold or heat, and having the same hour.

.

## Project 9. Manage all the oceans

**Description:** The objective of this project is to carefully manage all the oceans for all the people.

**Management**: All the leaders in the world, with the help of the United Nations.

**Start day:** 1 November 2020

**Completion day:** continuous

**Budget:** $45,000,000

**Results after implementation:** Saving lives, much better standards of living for all,
saving over $520,000,000/year in better fishing results, better navigation, etc.

**Comments:** The oceans are important for people and for our planet. All the oceans will belong to some of the regions, therefore will be maintained by those regions, to be free of any piracy or other bad activity – World Police will help when necessary.

Switzerland, Geneva (121 BC under Romans, 375 m elevation, population 200,000, area 16 km², 70 km northwest of Mont Blanc (4810 m)), Maison Royale (1909, a historic and artistic building ($8M) at 46 Quai Gustave Ador (1845-1928, President), and the name of a borough around it, southeast of the Jet d'Eau (1886, 1891, 1951)), southwest of Rue Jean-Henri Merle d'Aubigné (1794-1872, Swiss Protestant minister and historian of the Reformation).

# Project 10. Informing people about the World Government

**Description:** The objective of this project is to keep people correctly informed about the World Government, in order to improve it.

**Management**: All the teachers in the world, and the people.

**Start day:** 1 November 2020

**Completion day:** continuous

**Budget:** $255,000

**Results after implementation:** Saving millions of hours of documentation, much better-informed people,
saving over $78,000,000/year by having less bureaucracy, more productivity, etc.

**Comments:** It is important for people to know the World Government, in order to have peace, freedom, good health, harmony and prosperity. Peaceful Terra, with its family of over 7.7 B people, will have four levels of world management: at the local level, if needed, it could be one or two more levels of local managers (mayors, town managers, county managers – all levels of management must be friendly, helpful, fast, polite, modest and smart):

Level 1 Management: 1,000 L1 friendly managers, for the 1,000 districts, who will supervise and assist the mayors and town managers from their district, for a total of about 7,700,000 people in each district. Each of the 1,000 L1 friendly managers will be located in a central city from their districts – they could be the mayors of those cities, but with new responsibilities for the whole district.

Level 2 Management: 100 L2 friendly managers, for the 100 sub-regions, who will supervise and assist the 10 L1 managers of the 10 districts of each sub-region, for a total of about 77,000,000 people for each sub-region. These 100 L2 friendly managers will move each month between the two capitals of each of the 100 sub-regions.

Level 3 Management: 10 L3 friendly managers for the 10 regions.

Level 4 Management: 10 L4 friendly advisers for the world.

Italy, Naples (Napoli 1500 BC), Castel Nuovo (1282, called Maschio Angioino), in front of Piazza Municipio and the city hall.

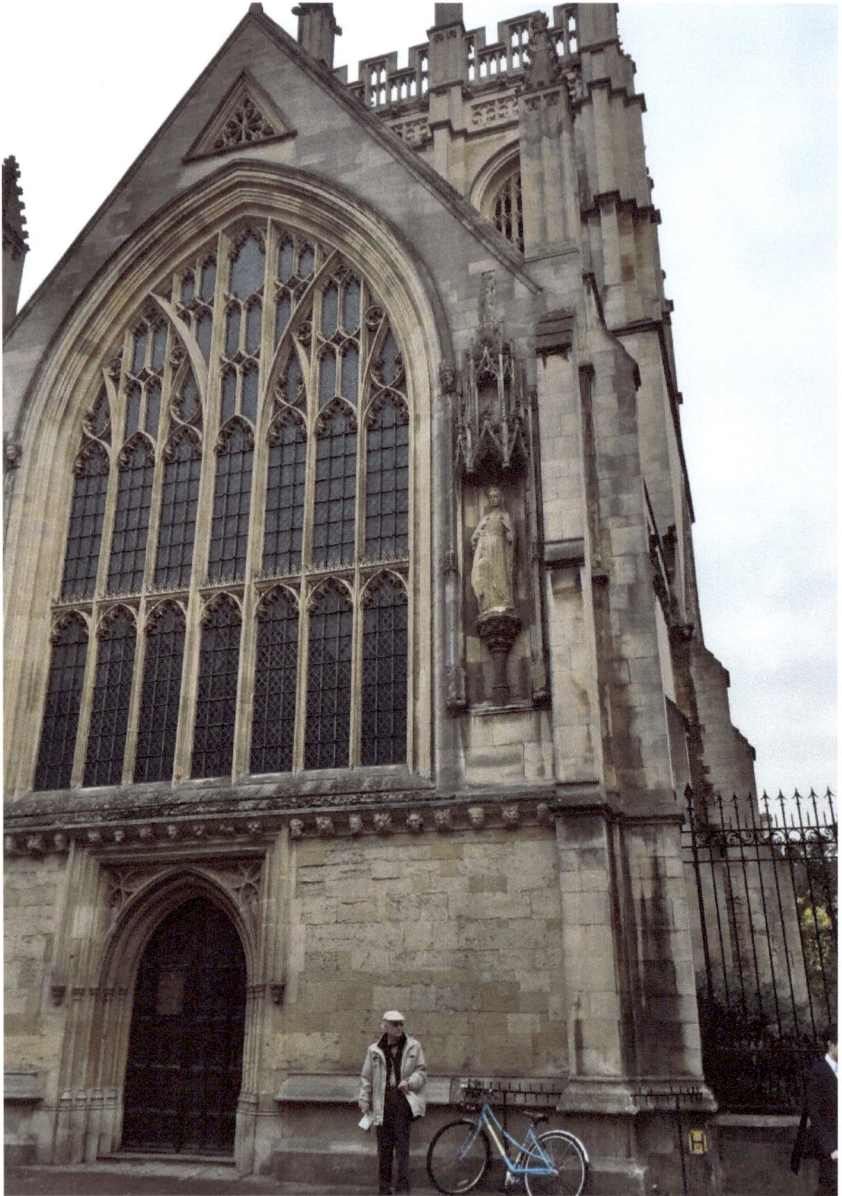

From Merton Street, looking southeast to the north (left) and west (right) facades of Merton College Chapel (1294, 1425, 1451, the church of Merton College (1264, the third oldest in Oxford)); there were plans to extend this church to the west (right), but the land was leased in 1517 to Bishop Richard Foxe (1448-1528), who founded Corpus Christy College (1517), next door (west) to Merton.

# Project 11. Prepare the two capitals for each sub-region

**Description:** The objective of this project is to prepare 200 cities to be sub-region capitals.

**Management**: All the leaders in the world, with the help of the United Nations.

**Start day:** 1 November 2020

**Completion day:** 1 September 2021

**Budget:** $60,000,000

**Results after implementation:** Saving millions of hours, much better standards of living for all,
saving over $1,330,000,000/year with cheaper locations, labor, etc.

**Comments:** It is relevant to have many cities refreshed and prepared to be capitals of sub-regions.
For example: in the beginning these capitals will be:

## In Region R0: from Paris (France) to N'Djamena (Chad)

- The sub-region R00 will have the capitals Paris (France) and Niamey (Niger) – assistance from Magdeburg (Germany).
- The sub-region R01 will have the capitals Brussels (Belgium) and Porto-Novo (Benin) - assistance from Toronto (Canada).
- The sub-region R02 will have the capitals Amsterdam (Netherlands) and Algiers (Algeria) - assistance from Graz (Austria).

- The sub-region R03 will have the capitals Luxembourg (Luxembourg) and Sao Tome (Sao Tome and Principe) - assistance from Adelaide (Australia).
- The sub-region R04 will have the capitals of Abuja (Nigeria) and Bochum (Germany) - assistance from Nikko (Japan).
- The sub-region R05 will have the capitals Malabo (Equatorial Guinea), and Zürich (Switzerland) - assistance from Leeds (UK).
- The sub-region R06 will have the capitals Oslo (Norway) and Tunis (Tunisia) - assistance from Sheffield (UK).
- The sub-region R07 will have the capitals Roma (Italy) and Luanda (Angola) - assistance from Yamagata (Japan).
- The sub-region R08 will have the capitals in Berlin (Germany) and Tripoli (Libya) - assistance from New York (USA).
- The sub-region R09 will have the capitals Prague (Czech Republic) and N'Djamena (Chad) - assistance from Brisbane (Australia).

Paris: Rue Soufflot (from Panthéon, looking north-west to Jardin du Luxembourg (1612, back), and Tour Eiffel (1889, 324 m)), with the Université Paris 1 Panthéon-Sorbonne (1150, 1971, right).

Italy, Rome: The Temple of Vesta and Rome and a flag throwing festival on 8 December 2011.

USA, New York: On W 42nd St, at Broadway, looking to Hilton Garden Inn (right, in a red building), and Times Square to the left.

## In Region R1: from Zagreb (Croatia) to Bujumbura (Burundi)

- The sub-region R10 will have the capitals in Zagreb (Croatia) and Brazzaville (Congo) - assistance from Nantes (France).
- The sub-region R11 will have the capitals in Vienna (Austria), Windhoek (Namibia) - assistance from Bilbao (Spain).
- The sub-region R12 will have the capitals in Stockholm (Sweden), Bangui (Central African Republic) - assistance from Florence (Italy).
- The sub-region R13 will have the capitals in Budapest (Hungary), Rundu (Namibia) - assistance from Monaco (Monaco).
- The sub-region R14 will have the capitals in Belgrade (Serbia), Kananga (Democratic Republic of Congo) - assistance from Liverpool (UK).
- The sub-region R15 will have the capitals in Athens (Greece), Mongu (Zambia) - assistance from Los Angeles (CA, USA).
- The sub-region R16 will have the capitals in Helsinki (Finland) and Kolwezi (Democratic Republic of the Congo) - assistance from Montreal (Canada).
- The sub-region R17 will have the capitals in Bucharest (Romania) and Gaborone (Botswana) - assistance from Philadelphia (PA, USA).
- The sub-region R18 will have the capitals in Minsk (Belarus) and Maseru (Lesotho) - assistance from Orleans (France).
- The sub-region R19 will have the capitals in Chisinau (Republic of Moldova) and Bujumbura (Burundi) - assistance from Hamburg (Germany).

Italy, Cividale del Friuli, 3 Nov 2009, on Largo Boiani, looking to il Duomo di Santa Maria Assunta (1457-1529, center left), Campanile (center right up), a statue down of Giulio Caesare (100 BC – 44 BC), signs to Castelmonte 9 km, and Gorizia 28 km.

USA, New York: On W 42$^{nd}$ St, the northeast façade of the New York Public Library (1902).

## In Region R2: from Kiev (Ukraine) to Baghdad (Iraq)

- The sub-region R20 will have the capitals in Kiev (Ukraine) and Kigali (Rwanda) - assistance from Ottawa (Canada).
- The sub-region R21 will have the capitals in Ankara (Turkey) and Khartoum (Sudan) - assistance from Salzburg (Austria).
- The sub-region R22 will have the capitals in Lilongwe (Malawi) and Nicosia (Cyprus) - assistance from Dallas (TX, USA).
- The sub-region R23 will have the capitals in Jerusalem (Israel) and Dodoma (Tanzania) - assistance from Strasbourg (France).
- The sub-region R24 will have the capitals in Damascus (Syria) and Nairobi (Kenya) - assistance from Stuttgart (Germany).
- The sub-region R25 will have the capitals in Krasnodar (Russia) and Addis Ababa (Ethiopia) - assistance from Marseille (France).
- The sub-region R26 will have the capitals in Rostov-on-Don (Russia) and Asmara (Eritrea) - assistance from Leipzig (Germany).
- The sub-region R27 will have the capitals in Stavropol (Russia) and Djibouti (Djibouti) - assistance from Zürich (Switzerland).
- The sub-region R28 will have the capitals in Mosul (Iraq) and Moroni (Comoros) - assistance from Linz (Austria).
- The sub-region R29 will have the capitals in Yerevan (Armenia) and Baghdad (Iraq) - assistance from Göttingen (Germany).

The upper part of the western façade of Cathédrale Notre Dame de
Paris (1163 – 1345, 90 m), on the south-eastern part of the Île de la
Cité, which is considered the center of Paris, in the fourth
arrondissement. The organ has 7,374 pipes, with about 900
classified as historical. It has 110 real stops, five 56-key manuals
and a 32-key pedalboard; it is now fully computerized. The Towers
at Notre-Dame contain five church bells. The great bourdon bell,
Emmanuel, from 1681, 13 t, is located in the South Tower (right).

## In Region R3: from Riyadh (Saudi Arabia) to Malé (Maldives)

- The sub-region R30 will have the capitals in Riyadh (Saudi Arabia) and Mogadishu (Somalia) - assistance from Bonn (Germany).
- The sub-region R31 will have the capitals in Baku (Azerbaijan) and Antananarivo (Madagascar) - assistance from Le Mans (France).
- The sub-region R32 will have the capitals in Oral (Kazakhstan) and Tehran (Iran) - assistance from Pisa (Italy).
- The sub-region R33 will have the capitals in Ashgabat (Turkmenistan) and Abu Dhabi (United Arab Emirates) - assistance from Wolfsburg (Germany).
- The sub-region R34 will have the capitals in Magnitogorsk (Russia) and Muscat (Oman) - assistance from Toulouse (France).
- The sub-region R35 will have the capitals in Chelyabinsk (Russia) and Herat (Afghanistan) - assistance from Basel (Switzerland).
- The sub-region R36 will have the capitals in Tyumen (Russia) and Kandahar (Afghanistan) - assistance from Nagoya (Japan).
- The sub-region R37 will have the capitals in Dushanbe (Tajikistan) and Labytnangi (Russia) - assistance from Limoges (France).
- The sub-region R38 will have the capitals in Tashkent (Uzbekistan) and Kabul (Afghanistan) - assistance from Rostock (Germany).
- The sub-region R39 will have the capitals in Islamabad (Pakistan) and Malé (Maldives) - assistance from La Rochelle (France).

6 April 1978, Pisa, Cattedrale di Pisa (1092, striped-marble, left), Torre di Pisa (August 1173-1372, 55.86 m on the low side, 56.67 m on the high side, white-marble, 296 steps, right).

Paris: Université Paris 1 Panthéon-Sorbonne (1971, after the division of the University of Paris (Sorbonne, 1150)), on Rue Saint-Jacques (left) and Rue Soufflot (right, to Panthéon (1758 – 1790)).

## In Region R4: from Bishkek (Kyrgyzstan) to Brahmapur (India)

- The sub-region R40 will have the capitals in Bishkek (Kyrgyzstan) and Jaipur (India) - assistance from Osaka (Japan).
- The sub-region R41 will have the capitals in Akola (India) and Kashgar (China) - assistance from Genoa (Italy).
- The sub-region R42 will have the capitals in Almaty (Kazakhstan) and Coimbatore (India) - assistance from Perth (Australia).
- The sub-region R43 will have the capitals in Kuybyshev (Russia) and Agra (India) - assistance from Fukuoka (Japan).
- The sub-region R44 will have the capitals in Vertikos (Russia) and Nagpur (India) - assistance from Coral Bay (Australia).
- The sub-region R45 will have the capitals in Chennai (India) and Colombo (Sri Lanka) - assistance from Sapporo (Japan).
- The sub-region R46 will have the capitals in Lucknow (India) and Fedosikha (Russia) - assistance from Niigata (Japan).
- The sub-region R47 will have the capitals in Bilaspur (India) and Kolpashevo (Russia) - assistance from Albany (Australia).
- The sub-region R48 will have the capitals in Visakhapatnam (India) and Barnaul (Russia) - assistance from Hiroshima (Japan).
- The sub-region R49 will have the capitals in Brahmapur (India) and Tomsk (Russia) - assistance from Yokohama (Japan).

Rome: Accademia Nazionale dei Lincei (1603) in Villa Farnesina
(1510). The author was invited to give a lecture here in 1977.

Switzerland, Lausanne (150), Place de la Navigation, the south side
of Hotel Aulac in a Belle Èpoque-style, near Château d'Ouchy.

## In Region R5: from Kathmandu (Nepal) to Dehong (China)

- The sub-region R50 will have the capitals in Kathmandu (Nepal) and Patna (India) - assistance from Kobe (Japan).
- The sub-region R51 will have the capitals in Bayingol (China) and Novokuznetsk (Russia) - assistance from Vichy (France).
- The sub-region R52 will have the capitals in Thimphu (Bhutan) and Dhaka (Bangladesh) - assistance from Jena (Germany).
- The sub-region R53 will have the capitals in Lhasa (China) and Achinsk (Russia) - assistance from Reims (France).
- The sub-region R54 will have the capitals in Abakan (Russia) and Kumul (China) - assistance from Fribourg (Switzerland).
- The sub-region R55 will have the capitals in Kyzyl (Russia) and Dibrugarh (India) - assistance from Denmark (Australia).
- The sub-region R56 will have the capitals in Bassein (Myanmar) and Tinsukia (India) - assistance from Chiba (Japan).
- The sub-region R57 will have the capitals in Yushu City (China) and Tinskoy (Russia) - assistance from Klagenfurt (Austria).
- The sub-region R58 will have the capitals in Jiuquan (China) and Medan (Indonesia) - assistance from Lucerne (Switzerland).
- The sub-region R59 will have the capitals in Chiang Mai (Thailand) and Dehong (China) - assistance from Mulhouse (France).

Switzerland, Geneva (121 BC under Romans, 375 m elevation, population 200,000, area 16 km², 70 km northwest of Mont Blanc (4810 m)), on Rue de la Servette (to the right, going southeast, Rue Jean Robert Chouet ((1642-1731, physician and politician) (the street is to the left, going northeast)), a nice building having down the restaurant Le Portail Chez Rui (yellow), 1.6 km northwest from Jet d'Eau, 1.6 km southwest from Palais des Nations (UN), 1.4 km northwest from the Université de Genève (1559, John Calvin (1509-1564)).

## In Region R6: from Bangkok (Thailand) to Chita (Russia)

- The sub-region R60 will have the capitals in Bangkok (Thailand) and Kuala Lumpur (Malaysia) - assistance from Besançon (France).
- The sub-region R61 will have the capitals in Vientiane (Laos) and Singapore – assistance from Freiburg im Breisgau (Germany).
- The sub-region R62 will have the capitals in Phnom Penh (Cambodia) and Irkutsk (Russia) – assistance from Baden (Switzerland).
- The sub-region R63 will have the capitals in Palembang (Indonesia), Hanoi (Vietnam) – assistance from Thun (Switzerland).
- The sub-region R64 will have the capitals in Ulan Bator (Mongolia) and Ulan-Ude (Russia) – assistance from Chaumont (France).
- The sub-region R65 will have the capitals in Cirebon (Indonesia) and Nanning (China) – assistance from Vaduz (Lichtenstein).
- The sub-region R66 will have the capitals in Pontianak (Indonesia) and Baotou (China) – assistance from Lugano (Switzerland).
- The sub-region R67 will have the capitals in Surakarta (Indonesia) and Yichang (China) – assistance from Thonon-les-Bain (France).
- The sub-region R68 will have the capitals in Surabaya (Indonesia) and Changsha (China) – assistance from Burgdorf (Switzerland).
- The sub-region R69 will have the capitals in Chita (Russia) and Hong Kong (China) – assistance from Colmar (France).

Italy, Rome: Piazza Venezia from Altare della Patria, Palazzo Venezia (1455).

Switzerland, Lausanne (Roman 150, 147,000, 41 km$^2$, 500 m elevation), marina on Lac Léman, Place de la Navigation (right).

## In Region R7: from Nanchang (China) to Melbourne (Australia)

- The sub-region R70 will have the capitals in Bandar Seri Begawan (Brunei Darussalam) and Nanchang (China) – assistance from Turku (Finland).
- The sub-region R71 will have the capitals in Krasnokamensk (Russia) and Jinan (China) – assistance from St. Gallen (Switzerland).
- The sub-region R72 will have the capitals in Baguio City (Philippines) and Hangzhou (China) – assistance from Dole (France).
- The sub-region R73 will have the capitals in Manila (Philippines) and Taipei (Taiwan, China) – assistance from Metz (France).
- The sub-region R74 will have the capitals in Kupang (Indonesia) and Shanghai (China) – assistance from Davos (Switzerland).
- The sub-region R75 will have the capitals in Pyongyang (North Korea) and Seoul (South Korea) – assistance from Versailles (France).
- The sub-region R76 will have the capitals in Vladivostok (Russia) and Busan (South Korea) – assistance from Innsbruck (Austria).
- The sub-region R77 will have the capitals in Kyoto (Japan) and Khabarovsk (Russia) – assistance from Germering (Germany).
- The sub-region R78 will have the capitals in Nagoya (Japan) and Komsomolsk-on-Amur (Russia) – assistance from Venice (Italy).
- The sub-region R79 will have the capitals in Sendai (Japan) and Melbourne (Australia) – assistance from St. Moritz (Switzerland).

Italy, 6 April 1978, Pisa, Palazzo della Carovana (1562-1564) now for Scuola Normale Superiore (1810, by Napoleon Bonaparte (1769-1821), 460 students, 6% admission rate, best in Italy).

Sweden, Malmö, from Skeppsbron looking north to the north part of the west side of the Central Station (right), sign for Trelleborg and Limhamn (to left), Goteborg and Hamnen (straight).

## In Region R8: from Anchorage (Alaska, USA) to Lima (Peru)

- The sub-region R80 will have the capitals in Uelen (Russia) and Anchorage (Alaska, USA), – assistance from Zug (Switzerland).
- The sub-region R81 will have the capitals in Vancouver (Canada) and San Jose (CA, USA) – assistance from Odense (Denmark).
- The sub-region R82 will have the capitals in Vernon (Canada) and Los Angeles (CA, USA) – assistance from Amstetten (Austria).
- The sub-region R83 will have the capitals in Calgary (Canada) and Tijuana (Mexico) – assistance from Chur (Switzerland).
- The sub-region R84 will have the capitals in Hermosillo (Mexico) and Tucson (AR, USA) – assistance from Bergen (Norway).
- The sub-region R85 will have the capitals in Chihuahua (Mexico) and Regina (Canada) – assistance from Gothenburg (Sweden).
- The sub-region R86 will have the capitals in San Luis Potosi City (Mexico) and Winnipeg (Canada) – assistance from Yverdon-les-Bains (Switzerland).
- The sub-region R87 will have the capitals in Tulsa (OK, USA) and Veracruz (Mexico) – assistance from Bregenz (Austria).
- The sub-region R88 will have the capitals in Memphis (TN, USA) and San José (Costa Rica) – assistance from Uppsala (Sweden).
- The sub-region R89 will have the capitals in Lima (Peru) and Boston (MA, USA) – assistance from Tampere (Finland).

USA, Boston, 3 Dec 2009, from Avenue Louis Pasteur (1822-1895, French microbiologist), Boston Public Latin School (1635, Schola Latina Bostoniensis, the oldest and the first public exam school in the U.S.).

Italy, Roma: Piazza Venezia and Altare della Patria or Il Monumento Nazionale (1911 -1925) a Vittorio Emanuele II..

## In Region R9: from La Paz (Bolivia) to London (United Kingdom)

- The sub-region R90 will have the capitals in La Paz (Bolivia) and Bangor (Maine, USA) – assistance from Aosta (Italy).
- The sub-region R91 will have the capitals in Caracas (Venezuela) and Road Town (British Virgin Islands) – assistance from Obergoms (Switzerland).
- The sub-region R92 will have the capitals in Buenos Aires (Argentina) and Fort-de-France (Martinique) – assistance from Freudenstadt (Germany).
- The sub-region R93 will have the capitals in Asuncion (Paraguay) and Montevideo (Uruguay) – assistance from Winterthur (Switzerland).
- The sub-region R94 will have the capitals in Cayenne (French Guiana), St. John's (Canada) – assistance from Novara (Italy).
- The sub-region R95 will have the capitals in Rio de Janeiro (Brazil) and Dakar (Senegal) – assistance from Toyama (Japan).
- The sub-region R96 will have the capitals in Freetown (Sierra Leone) and Lisbon (Portugal) – assistance from Kawasaki (Japan).
- The sub-region R97 will have the capitals in Bamako (Mali) and Athlone (Ireland) – assistance from Ulm (Germany).
- The sub-region R98 will have the capitals in Yamoussoukro (Cote d'Ivoire) and Madrid (Spain) – assistance from Okayama (Japan).
- The sub-region R99 will have the capitals in Ouagadougou (Burkina Faso) and London (United Kingdom) - assistance from Vaasa (Finland).

Looking northwest to the southeast side of the South Building (1899, Astronomy Center) of Royal Observatory Greenwich (1676).

USA, Cambridge, 23 September 2009, on the campus of Harvard University (1636) in Cambridge, The Harry Elkins Widener (1885-1912 (died on Titanic)) Memorial Library (1915, Beaux-Arts architecture, 3.5 M of books).

## Project 12. Informing people about the Level 3 Management

**Description:** The objective of this project is to make people familiar with this Level 3 Management.

**Management**: All the teachers in the world, with the help of some managers.

**Start day:** 1 November 2020

**Completion day:** 12 July 2021

**Budget:** $540,000

**Results after implementation:** Saving millions of hours of documentation, much better standards of living for all,
saving over $58,000,000/year with improved management, efficiency, people involvement, etc.

**Comments:** It is useful to have informed people. The ten L3 friendly managers for the 10 regions will supervise and assist the 10 L2 managers of the 10 sub-regions of each region, for a total of about 770,000,000 people for each region.
        For example, the Region R0 will have the first capitals in

## Bern (Switzerland) and Libreville (Gabon) – assistance from Oxford (UK).

For better quality and consistency of the management, we'll have the first two cities from the region R0, and the third city from outside. Actually, being inside the same country Terra, any city, sub-region or region can ask for advice or help from anybody.

    - The Region R1 will have the first capitals in

**Warsaw (Poland) and Pretoria (South Africa) – assistance from Miami (FL, USA).**

- The Region R2 will have the first capitals in

**Moscow (Russia) and Cairo (Egypt) – assistance from Grenoble (France).**

- The Region R3 will have the first capitals in

**Astana (Kazakhstan) and Karachi (Pakistan), – assistance from Montpellier (France).**

Paris: Place de la Concorde (Louis XV, 1772, 359 m by 212 m, 8.64 ha), with sumptuous light poles.

- The Region R4 will have the first capitals in

**New Delhi (India) and Novosibirsk (Russia) – assistance from Magdeburg (Germany).**

- The Region R5 will have the first capitals in

**Krasnoyarsk (Russia) and Urumqi (China) – assistance from Avignon (France).**

- The Region R6 will have the first capitals in

**Jakarta (Indonesia) and Beijing (China) – assistance from Neuchâtel (Switzerland).**

- The Region R7 will have the first capitals in

**Tokyo (Japan) and Sydney (Australia) – assistance from Malmö (Sweden).**

- The Region R8 will have the first capitals in

**Washington (USA) and Mexico City (Mexico) – assistance from Bellinzona (Switzerland).**

- The Region R9 will have the first capitals in

**Halifax (Canada) and Brasilia (Brazil) – assistance from Biel (Switzerland).**

France, Paris, the north-west part of L'Institut de France (1795, moved in 1805 by Napoléon in this baroque building from 1684) is a revered French cultural society with five académies, the most famous being Académie Français (1635) and. Académie des sciences (1666).

UK, London, at the east end of Westminster Bridge (1862, 250 m, width 26 m, 7 spans, right) over Thames (flowing left to right), Palace of Westminster (1016, 1870, 300 m river front façade, 1,100 rooms, center left, with Victoria Tower (1858, 98 m, left), and Central Tower (91 m)), Big Ben (Elizabeth Tower, 1855, 96 m, center right).

## Project 13. Informing people about the Level 4 Management

**Description:** The objective of this project is to make people familiar with this Level 4 Management.

**Management**: All the teachers in the world, with the help of some managers.

**Start day:** 1 November 2020

**Completion day:** 1 February 2021

**Budget:** $430,000

**Results after implementation:** Saving millions of hours of documentation, much better standards of living for all,
saving over $634,000,000/year with better management, direct communication, improved efficiency, etc.

**Comments:** It is really important to know well to top management. The level 4 Management are the very friendly 10 Advisers of the world will supervise and assist the 10 L3 managers of the 10 regions of the Earth, for a total of about 7,700,000,000 people – all the people on Earth, citizens of Peaceful Terra.

# Project 14. Preparing locations for the 10 Advisors

**Description:** The objective of this project is to transform many cities by having advisors located there.

**Management**: Many leaders in the world, with the help of the people.

**Start day:** 1 November 2020

**Completion day:** 11 May 2021

**Budget:** $340,000

**Results after implementation:** Saving millions of hours of documentation, much better standards of living for all, saving over $720,000/year with cheaper cities, better management, people involvement, less bureaucracy, etc.

**Comments:** It is an easy and simple project, but important. The 10 Advisors will be located each in one the ten Regions R0, R1,…, R9. For example, in the beginning, for the first month (then changing every month), the ten Advisers of the world will be located:

- in R0: Barcelona (Spain)
- in R1: Benghazi (Libya)
- in R2: Addis Ababa (Ethiopia)
- in R3: Hyderabad (Pakistan)
- in R4: Bhopal (India)
- in R5: Mandalay (Myanmar)
- in R6: Nanchong (China)
- in R7: Khabarovsk (Russia)
- in R8: Houston (USA)
- in R9: Recife (Brazil)

These ten L4 Advisers will be in permanent contact with each other, and with the L3 Advisers, for the best management of the world.

The ten L4 Advisers will move each month from a first capital of a region to the second capital of another region, at random (or based on urgency, if an emergency occurred). This mobility is essential for having a long period of tranquility and harmony.

The Advisors will be located in the current government buildings, and the excess government buildings and properties will be sold, in order to increase the budget, and to reduce the expenses.

Italy, Roma: The south-west side of the Amphitheatrum Flavium (Colosseum, 80 AD), with a flag throwing festival on December 8, 2011.

# Project 15. Preparing technical equipment for the 10 Advisors

**Description:** The objective of this project is to have good equipment for the top 10 Advisers (and all the others), who will collaborate via e-mail, telephone, videoconferences, mail, or face to face, when needed, to produce practical results for all people, very fast.

**Management**: Good engineers from the world, with the help of the United Nations.

**Start day:** 1 November 2020

**Completion day:** 18 January 2021

**Budget:** $5,600,000

**Results after implementation:** Saving millions of hours of unproductive work,
saving over $58,000,000/year with improved communication, better management, etc.

**Comments:** It is essential to have advanced systems for the top management. The ten L4 Advisers will work by consensus only. It is expected that the 10 Advisors are talented enough to be able to negotiate fast any disagreements between them, and quickly arrive at the best common decision, for the benefit of all people.

## Project 16. Preparing elections for the 10 Advisors

**Description:** The objective of this project is to have quiet and civilized elections for the top management.

**Management**: CEOs of good companies, with the help of the doctors, mathematicians, engineers, teachers and the United Nations.

**Start day:** 1 November 2020

**Completion day:** 1 August 2021

**Budget:** $3,570,000

**Results after implementation:** Saving millions of people from bad management, creating conditions for much better standards of living for all,
saving over $866,000,000/year by eliminating bad propaganda, by encouraging honesty and modesty, etc.

**Comments:** It is a high priority to have good, calm and friendly elections.
        The ten L4 Advisers will be elected from the 10 regions, and each of them will be the First Adviser (***First among equals*** – from Latin: Primus inter pares) for one month, by rotation.
        The First Adviser only coordinates the work of the other 9 Advisors for one month.

# Project 17. Distributing reports from the 10 Advisors?

**Description:** The objective of this project is to keep people informed about the activities of the top 10 Advisors.

**Management**: Good engineers from the world, with the help of the United Nations.

**Start day:** 1 June 2021

**Completion day:** continuous

**Budget:** $7,600,000/year

**Results after implementation:** Saving millions of hours of non-useful work, having informed people,
saving over $643,000,000/year in unnecessary reporting techniques, providing better and faster necessary reports, etc.

**Comments:** It is imperative to correctly inform people by using a Monthly World Report.

The First Adviser, on the last day of each month, will present in writing for the world (no more than 5 standard pages) a clear and precise Monthly World Report, with a list of finished and unfinished tasks.

The other 9 Advisers will add their comments to the Monthly World Report (no more than half a page each - total report less than 9.5 pages).

In order to better know the world government, to help it, and, especially, to improve it, all able people of the world will work as volunteers at least one day per year in each of the seven departments.

After each Monthly World Report, a public opinion survey about the report should be taken, and presented to all Advisors.

Italy, sunset on the Tyrrhenian Sea, in Fregene, near the Fiumicino Airport, 25 km west of Rome.

Switzerland, Lausanne (Roman 150, 147,000, 41 km$^2$, 500 m elevation), marina on Lac Léman, Place de la Navigation (right).

# Project 18. Recording all Advisors' decisions

**Description:** The objective of this project is to record all activities of the Advisors, and others from the small World Government, to be available to the people on a website.

**Management**: Good engineers from the world, with the help of other people.

**Start day:** 1 July 2020

**Completion day:** 1 November 2021

**Budget:** $3,570,000

**Results after implementation:** Saving millions of hours of clerical work, having informed people,
saving over $96,700,000/year with fast and calm recording, no unnecessary work, promoting advanced technology, etc.

**Comments:** The decisions must be ready for use by all people. The top 10 Advisers will manage Police and all other Departments. All the activities of all Advisors will be recorded in computers and videos, and on paper, for people to be able to see what they are doing. All Advisors are free to speak about their administrative work, with modesty.

## Project 19. Elimination of war mentality

**Description:** The objective of this project is simply to eliminate the war mentality, in order to help all the people on Earth to live better, peacefully, free, healthy, and prosperous.

**Management**: All the teachers in the world, with the help of the people.

**Start day:** 1 November 2020

**Completion day:** continuous

**Budget:** $200,000

**Results after implementation:** Saving millions of people from the stress of war, much better standards of living for all, saving over $46,870,000/year by reducing medical expenses, improving the happiness, etc.

**Comments:** It is an important effort, useful for everybody. Advisors (and all the others) cannot declare war, reprisals or capture land or water. Advisors (and all the others) cannot raise and support armies, navy, or any military forces.

# Project 20. Prepare the 5 assistants

**Description:** The objective of this project is to prepare the 5 assistants for all managers.

**Management**: Doctors, mathematicians, CEOs, engineers and teachers from the world, with the help of other people.

**Start day:** 1 November 2020

**Completion day:** continuous

**Budget:** $62,000/year

**Results after implementation:** Saving millions of hours of unnecessary work, much better standards of living for all,
saving over $751,000,000/year by eliminating many bureaucratic activities, revitalizing good government performance, improving services for all people.

**Comments:** It is a sine qua non requirement to have highly qualified professional to help the government to deliver good services to the population. Each Advisor, and each manager at all levels, will have 5 immediate assistants:
1) a mathematician for finance and all other calculations,
2) a medical doctor for keeping everybody healthy, calm, polite, friendly and optimist,
3) a CEO for good management,
4) an engineer for all practical projects, and
5) a teacher for education, training and related areas.
      The five assistants play a key role, because they are highly qualified professionals, who actually will carry on the practical management of the world.
      The five assistants' integrity, professionalism and friendliness will significantly improve the quality of the world and local governments.

The five assistants are really the experts. They will assist the Advisors and all levels of management, in order to have an efficient, correct and professional working of the world government at all levels.

All spending proposals from Advisers must be approved by their 5 assistants (doctors, mathematicians, CEOs, engineers and teachers), and must have an already existing funding in the budget.

3 Dec 2009, from Harvard Medical School looking northeast to the Avenue Louis Pasteur (1822-1895, French microbiologist),

## Project 21. Preparing elections for the Honorific World Observer

**Description:** The objective of this project is to have quiet and civilized elections for this very special top management.

**Management**: CEOs of good companies, with the help of the doctors, mathematicians, engineers, teachers and the United Nations.

**Start day:** 1 June 2021

**Completion day:** 1 November 2021

**Budget:** $2,600,000

**Results after implementation:** Saving millions of hours of irrelevant work, moving on the road towards much better standards of living for all,
saving over $356,000,000/year by eliminating bureaucratic work, helping people to understand the importance of good government, etc.

**Comments:** Serious attention must be given to this process, because of its special importance. An Honorific World Observer will be quietly elected by direct vote – starting, for example, 1$^{st}$ September 2022 - for only one 3 years term, with the main duty to observe that the top 10 Advisers efficiently perform their duties, and keep their words – if they don't, they will be changed. For managers and for everybody else, keeping their word is a serious and strict requirement.
    The Honorific World Observer has this responsibility for the top 10 Advisors, but all people will pay attention to this. Words must become again important and respected.

France, Paris: La Monnaie de Paris (the Direction of Coins and Medals) created in 864 by Charles II (823-877, king 843-877), is the oldest French institution, which is still active. It also has a Musée de la Monnaie (1833), at 11 Quai de Conti, in the 6th arrondissement.

# Project 22. Logistics for the World Government

**Description:** The objective of this project is to help with the logistics for the World Government in order to work better.

**Management**: CEOs from the world, with the help of the United Nations.

**Start day:** 1 November 2020

**Completion day:** 1 November 2021

**Budget:** $70,000,000

**Results after implementation:** Saving millions of hours wasted on bureaucratic activities, much better standards of living for all, saving over $920,000,000/year from increased productivity, smooth operations, less bureaucracy, etc.

**Comments:** The World Government needs to be very efficient and economic – all people want this plus peace, freedom, good health, harmony and prosperity.

The World Government will have only 7 Departments, and there are some other important details:

All the employees of the World Government are temporary, and must reapply for their positions every year.

There is no need for unions.

The World Government will be limited to:

1) the Office of the Honorific Observer (less than 10 employees),
2) the Office of the top ten Advisors (less than 100 employees), and
3) 7 small departments.

Australia: A big and old tree in the Royal Botanic Gardens, south of the Sydney Opera House, with the Sydney Harbour (center left).

Paris (founded circa 250 BC): L'Hôtel National des Invalides (1678), in the 7th arrondissement, with military museums (including details about Lafayette) and monuments, and the burial site for Napoleon Bonaparte, 1769-1821.

# Project 23. Maintenance of the 7 World Government Departments

**Description:** The objective of this project is to provide maintenance work for the World Government.

**Management:** Good engineers from the world, with the help of others.

**Start day:** 1 November 2020

**Completion day:** continuous

**Budget:** $76,000,000/year

**Results after implementation:** Saving millions of hours of bureaucratic work, good government work to have much better standards of living for all,
saving over $930,000,000/year by improving productivity, better services for people, less waste, etc.

**Comments:** It is a matter of common sense – the World Government needs good maintenance and improvements, in order to have for all people peace, freedom, good health, harmony and prosperity.
    5.8.4 - The World Government will have these 7 small departments:

## - Tax Department

- Collects taxes of 15% of the income of people and revenue of companies.

- The Manager of the Tax Department is appointed for a three-year term by the World 10 Advisers.

- The number of employees must be under 50,000, with excellent computers, and advanced software.

USA, New York: On Broadway at 43<sup>rd</sup> St, looking southwest, in Times Square

## - Treasury

Treasury will control all the financial issues, including:
- antitrust
- fiscal service
- financial cooperation
- financing bank
- world reserve system
- world budget using only revenue, no borrowing, and spending only on strict necessary needs
– all the budgets, at all levels, will have a 2% surplus, which will be returned to the taxpayers
- register of all government papers and activities
- archives and records
- assist all people to have savings accounts for old age (the old age will be starting around 70), and 10% of their income should automatically go to their savings accounts. For those unable to work, their doctors and mathematicians will decide case by case.
- bankruptcies, in general, will be discouraged, and when strict necessary, will be analyzed and solved, case by case, by the doctors, mathematicians and CEOs who worked with the people who asked the bankruptcy.
- encourage all families to assist their parents, grandparents, and great-grandparents.
- housing finance
- housing for all people
- no homelessness
- consumer financial protection
- pensions
- privacy
- current social security until replaced by personal savings
- personnel management
- general services for the world government
- each the 10 regions will receive 2.5% of the world taxes - at least 30% of the money will be sent to villages and cities.
- each of the 100 sub-regions will receive 0.25% of the world taxes. At least 40% of the money will be sent to villages and cities.

- The World Central Bank will include all current central banks –
starting, for example, on May 1st, 2023.
- The Special Credit Card (SCC) will be issued by the World Central
Bank.
- Advisors will create a new world currency, named, for example,
"coin", and all the other currencies will be exchanged for coins. The
World Central Bank will implement the details.
- The counterfeiting and all other bad things, which some sick
people do, will be medically treated (in specialized medical
institutions when necessary), and those who did bad things will pay
all the expenses, and will reimburse the victims. Victims will always
be very protected, and helped to recover the losses from the
attackers.

Chiesa degli Scalzi (the church of Santa Maria di Nazareth) was
built by Baltassarre Longhena in 1654, and the façade made by
Giuseppe Sardi is the only one in Venice built with Carrara marble.

## - People Assistance Department

It will assist people in general, including:
- parent assistance
- dispute resolution
- in very simple disputes or culpa levis (ordinary negligence, like late payments, etc.), one single assistant will decide within minutes, and all people will go back to work
- census every 5 years
- election assistance every 20 months
 - special credit cards
- people protection against abuses from anybody
- completely eliminate corruption, organized crime and drug trafficking
- all people in the world will remain in their places, and the improvements will come to them. Those who want to move to other places, will need first a special invitation from at least 10 people (not family related) where they want to move.
- all the Tribunals and related areas will be transformed in people assistance services, based on friendliness, collaboration and goodwill.
- It is well understood that no excessive bail will be required, no excessive fines imposed, no cruel and unusual punishments applied, but, at the same time, it is well understood that a person who did a bad thing will receive the necessary corrective medical treatment, and will reimburse all people who suffered damages, and the medical treatment. The victims will always receive special attention.
- Nobility (King, Prince, etc.) could continue to exist in some places, but they should not interfere with activities of the Advisors, and actually should help them.
- food safety
- trash & recycling
- free commerce
- jobs assistance
- postal service
- labor safety and harmonious relations
- land, water

- volunteers
- fitness, sport, tourism
- 10 world holidays: the normal 4 Earth events (2 solstices (around 21 June, around 21 December), and 2 equinoxes (around 21 March, around 21 September), Mother's Day on 1$^{st}$ May, Father's Day on 6 August, Children's Day on 6 November, Grandparents' Day on 6 February, and 2 optional days (like Thanksgiving or a Religious Day (Christmas), and New Year).

Switzerland, from Genève to Thoiry (France), on Route de Meyrin, 2 km west from Geneva Cointrin Airport, there is this renovation of the external structural Elements of the Globe of Science and Innovation.

## - Medical Department

It will manage all medical and healthcare related areas, including:
- human services
- conflict resolution
- families, children, elderly
- medicine approval
- disease control and prevention
- medical doctors and assistants will make regular home visits, at least once a year, to all people, to keep them healthy, and to prevent illnesses.
- medical research: cancer, heart, lung, blood, arthritis, surgical robotics, connected computers for healthcare, etc.
- healthy homes, streets, stores, working places, etc.
- healthy aging
- all misunderstandings, disagreements or conflicts of any nature will be treated by medical personnel (with police help when strict necessary), until all is back to normal.
- no prisons are necessary, only specialized medical institutions (in simple cases, the places where the treated people live can be used, with the necessary limitations and surveillance)
- If a person X is considered that did a bad thing, X will have, within 3 days, a discussion with one or more doctors and other assistants, and will be informed of the nature and cause of the bad thing; including witnesses against and for him. Then a decision will be taken within other 3 days, by a group of doctors and other assistants. Victims of bad people will always have priority to discuss their problems with one or more doctors and other assistants, and quick decisions will be taken within 3 days, by a group of doctors and other assistants. Protection of victims has always priority.
- in order to better know the world government, to help it, and, especially, to improve it, all able people of the world will work as volunteers at least one day per year in the local facility of this department, which will have a special office for managing this volunteer work.

– all people will have government medical insurance, and they can also have private medical insurance

– there will be doctors working for the government 100%, or only part-time, or having only private practice, all with reasonable salaries and fees.

– there will be government pharmaceutical institutions and private pharmaceutical companies, offering reasonable priced medicines, without advertising to the general public.

Palazzo Giustinian (left), Piazza San Marco (center), Palazzo Ducale (center-right), seen from the east end of Canal Grande.

## - Police

Police will provide assistance for:
- accidents
- disasters
- complete elimination of nuclear, chemical and biological arms, firearms and explosives
- world complete security
- world cooperation
- conflict reduction and resolution
- investigations
- emergency assistance
- training
- delinquency prevention in general, and especially juvenile
- protection of Advisors, important government buildings, etc.
- extended surveillance and reconnaissance to prevent bad events
- fire protection
- volunteers to help police
- police will be present at public meetings, services, shows, etc., in order to protect the public
- public order
- ensuring traffic safety
- completely eliminate corruption, organized crime and drug trafficking
- movement of people based on civilized rules
- assist and protect those who have encountered violence
- World Police and specialists from the former United Nations and Interpol will be ready and very mobile for urgent and special operations, when they are needed.
- Police will be the only department which will have some small arms, in order to stop some very bad people (who are very sick).
- a small manufacturing and maintenance of arms unit will be part of the Police Department, under strict control.
- Police will work with medical personnel, mathematicians, CEOs, engineers, teachers and others, to make sure that all the people on the Planet are in good mental health, in order to prevent bad situations. This is also a major responsibility of all Advisors.

- prevention of bad events
- The Advisors will allocate the necessary budget for Police, and Police will assist people in need.

Italy, Rome (753 BC, one of the oldest continuously occupied cities in Europe, called Roma Aeterna (The Eternal City) and Caput Mundi (Capital of the World)), in Piazza Quirinale, the northeast side of Fountain of Castor (1818), with Obelisco del Quirinale (or Monte Cavallo, 1786, 29 m, from Mausoleum of Augustus (63 BC-14 AD)), and statues of the Dioscuri (Castor and Pollux, twin sons of Zeus and Leda) from the thermal baths of Constantine (272-337), Opus Phidiai on the left.

## - Education Department

- Over 2 billions of children in the world will get a solid peace-oriented education, to give a solid peace-oriented foundation for a good, free, peaceful and prosperous life.
- Education is very important – teachers will work with parents and grandparents, to educate the children to leave healthy in a sustainable peace, liberty and prosperity.
- Discipline must be strict, and those who do not behave properly, will get medical assistance.
- The world will have 4 school levels (SLs) of education:
SL1 – Kindergarten – 2 years: age 5 and 6
SL2 – Primary School – 4 years: age 7, 8, 9 and 10
SL3 – Secondary School – 3 years: age 11, 12 and 13
SL4 – High School or Vocational School – 4 years: age 14, 15, 16 and 17
- A World Library will include the Library of Congress and all the other great libraries – they will remain where they are now, but will be digitally interconnected, and accessible from any place in the world.
- adult education: technical, career
- training for employment
- management training
- post high school education
- peace education
- world constitution education

USA, Boston: a beautiful tall ship on the north-west side of the Boston Fish Pier. Bostonians welcome tall ships and their crews and cadets, from all over the world, to their harbor, on a continuous basis.

## - Science & Technology Department.

It will help in the areas of:
- mathematics
- statistics
- science
- technology
- Algorithmic Governance will be an essential tool for a better and impartial governing of the world, used by the Advisers elected by people. Mathematicians from all countries will work to improve the Algorithmic Governance, to better serve the people.
- cyberspace complete security will be achieved and strictly maintained
- information systems
- computer services
- Internet
- scientific cooperation
- economic development at the world level
- infrastructure improvement and maintenance at the world level
- innovation and improvements in all areas, at the world level
- transportation at the world level
- safety
- security
- aviation
- highway
- cars
- railroads without noise
- maritime administration
- logistics
- strategic planning at the world level
- public works
- fleet maintenance
- standards: weights, measures, etc.
- research at the world level
- risk analysis
- laboratories
- engineering

- communications at the world level
- telecommunications
- networks
- peaceful nuclear energy use at the world level
- safety
- waste
- electrical power
- oceanic analysis at the world level
- atmospheric analysis at the global level
- meteorological service and prognosis at the global level
- world resources analysis
- sustainable use of world resources
- geographical and geological activity
- product safety at the global level
- hazardous material and chemical safety
- government broadcasting (radio, tv, Internet, newspaper, etc.) including news, scientific and technical information
- private broadcasting will continue, but the world government must be able to directly inform the people, without intermediaries
- space exploration and expansion at the world level – very important for the future
- patent and trademark
- intellectual rights
- all government work, which can be done by private companies, will be contracted with the best and reasonably priced private companies. At the same time, the government should always have competitive services for people – from plumbing and electrical help, to mortgage and buying or selling a house.

# Project 24. Administration of elections

**Description:** The objective of this project is to provide good and impartial administration of all the elections.

**Management**: CEOs, doctors, from the world, with the help of the United Nations.

**Start day:** 1 November 2020

**Completion day:** continuous

**Budget:** $47,000,000/year

**Results after implementation:** Saving millions of hours of inefficient work, helping to have calm and friendly elections, saving over $320,000,000/year with simplified procedures, less bureaucracy, etc.

**Comments:** Obviously, calm and friendly elections are needed, and their good administration is essential. Political ad spending is over $6.7 B per election, therefore people's money is transferred to local TV – not good for people. Elections every 20 months.

The Advisers will be elected every 20 months for one term only. If an Adviser X was elected for a term T1, then the next term T2 will have another Advisor Y. For the next term T3, X can be elected again, but the next term T4 will have a new Adviser, and so on. All levels of Advisers (minimum age 25 years) can be elected, not consecutively, at most 4 times (maximum 80 months = 6 years and 8 months).

Advisers should have exceptional results obtained from their work, and based on these results, plus modesty, moderation, good character, friendliness, sharp mind, wisdom, good morals, and intense desire to help people, they will be elected, without any campaigning, publicity, fundraising, donations, debates, propaganda, political parties, advertising, or similar activities.

There will be use of advanced digital technology, which opens up entirely new opportunities for developing direct elections, and public control of the institutions, improving the transparency of the election procedure, and taking into account the interests and opinions of each voter (over the age of 21, who are not in a special medical institution for bad behavior or for mental health).

Italy, Rome (753 BC), Forum Romanum, the south half of the northwest side of Arcus Septimii Severi (left, 203, Septimius Severus (145 – 211)), the northeast side of Temple Saturni (center right, 497 BC, 42 BC, 380), Basilica Juliae (center back, 54 BC by Julius Caesar (100 – 44 BC), fluted Corinthian Column of Phocas (center left, 350 BC, 13 m, rededicated 1 August 608 to the Eastern (Byzantine) Roman Emperor Flavius Phocas (born 547, Emperor 602-610), the last Imperial monument in this Forum).

UK, London: From the northeast corner of Trafalgar Square, south of the National Gallery, looking southwest to Vice Admiral Horatio Nelson's (1758-1805 (aged 47), buried at St Paul's Cathedral) Column, and the equestrian statue of King George IV (1762-1830 (aged 68), King 1820-1830, patron of architecture, the eldest son of King George III (1738-1820 (aged 81), Reign 1760-1820 (59 years), during his reign, the American colonies created the U. S. A.)).

# Project 25. Checking of qualifications

**Description:** The objective of this project is to check the qualifications of those who want to run for elections.

**Management**: CEOs, doctors, scientists, teachers and others from the world.

**Start day:** 1 November 2020

**Completion day:** continuous

**Budget:** $4,000,000/year

**Results after implementation:** Saving millions of hours of superfluous work, much better management,
saving over $21,000,000/year by eliminating unqualified candidates, making sure that only people who want to serve all the people are included, etc.

**Comments:** Very important to have well qualified elected managers. This is the Election Commission of 110 representatives from the 10 regions and from the 100 sub-regions, elected separately for 5 years, will have to examine the qualifications of all the candidates for Advisers, and for other senior management positions. Unqualified candidates will be asked to improve their qualifications, and then to try again later.

It is important to refresh the management, and to bring new people to help the big family of 7.7 B people. The older generations, who performed well, will be retained in important roles, because experience and maturity count very much. At least two months before the retirement, they will kindly be asked to transfer their expertise to the younger generation. Even after retirement, they will occasionally be invited to share their expertise.

In every election, with every winner, will be other two for number 2 and number 3. The number 2 and number 3 for each management position will be used when number 1 is not available (vacation, sick, etc.). They will constantly work for number 1, helping to solve urgent problems for the people.

Good elections are essential for the future.

There has been a tendency to make elections conflict generating events, with lots of propaganda, false information, heavy donations, unpolite confrontations, bully fundraising, hostile political parties and organizations, unlimited power ambitions, etc.

This will be completely changed into clean, friendly elections, in which people choose between leaders with outstanding results, plus talent to lead people to peace and freedom, modesty, moderation, good character, friendliness, sharp mind, wisdom, good morals, and intense desire to help people – no campaigning, no publicity, no fundraising, no donations, no debates, no propaganda, no political parties, no advertising, or similar activities.

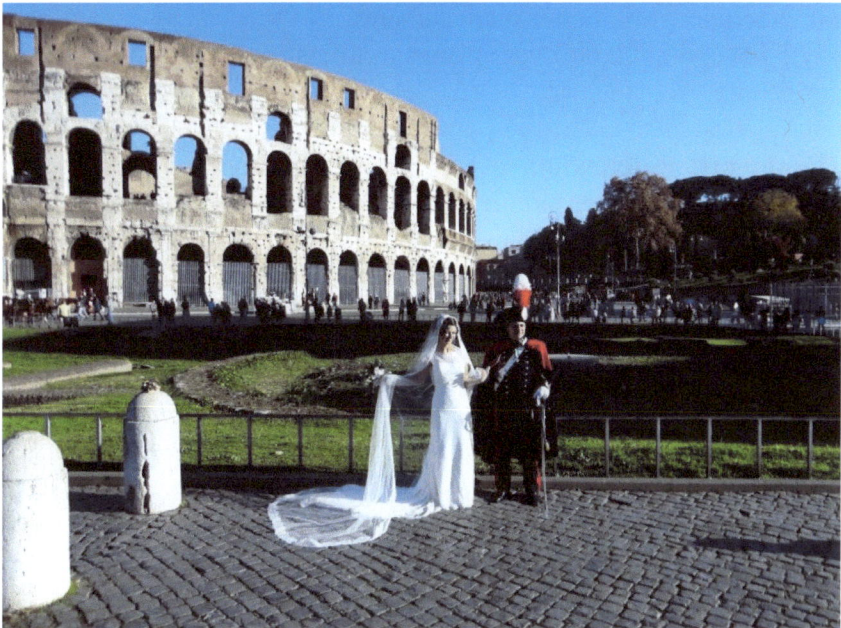

Rome: The south-west side of the Amphitheatrum Flavium (Colosseum, 80 AD) and a carabiniere wedding photo event.

# Project 26. Referendum administration

**Description:** The objective of this project is to administer all referenda.

**Management**: CEOs, doctors, mathematicians, teachers and others from the world.

**Start day:** 1 February 2021

**Completion day:** continuous

**Budget:** $7,000,000/year

**Results after implementation:** Saving millions of hours of bureaucratic work, better management,
saving over 40,000,000/year from simplification of work, faster help for people, etc.

**Comments:** Referendum is a necessity for good government. An electronic world referendum will be organized every three months. The main questions will be:
1. Are you satisfied with the Government?
2. What Government work is good?
3. What Government work is not good?
4: Suggestions for improvement:

Within two months after each referendum, the Government will respond to the people. Based on the suggestions received, new pro-people rules will be replacing some old rules.

Switzerland, Geneva, from Quai Gustave Ador (1845-1928, President). Jet d'Eau (1886, 1891, 1951) – a large fountain pumping lake water at 500 liters/s to 140 m, lit up at night. It is located at the point where Lac Léman empties into the Rhône River. There are two 500 kW pumps, operating at 2,400 V, consuming one megawatt of electricity. The water leaves the nozzle (10.16 cm) at a speed of 200 km/h. At any time, there are about 7,000 liters of water in the air.

## Project 27. Complete disarmament monitoring

**Description:** The objective of this project is to carefully monitor the complete disarmament on the Planet.

**Management**: Specialized police department, scientists, and other specialists from the world, with the help of the United Nations.

**Start day:** 1 November 2020

**Completion day:** continuous

**Budget:** $160,000,000/year

**Results after implementation:** Saving millions of lives, much better standards of living for all,
saving over $942,000,000/year with less bureaucracy, less warry, happier lives, etc.

**Comments:** It is a matter of common sense – all people want complete disarmament, peace, freedom, good health, harmony and prosperity.
        There will be no arms at all:
        Arms will not exist anymore, and only the police will have some small arms. Those who want arms for hunting or sport, will borrow them from police stations, with proper documents, rules and payments.
        All military units will become strong civilian organizations, working to improve the quality of life for everybody.
        A continuous verification and monitoring will be implemented, the make sure that the world finally achieved complete disarmament.

# Project 28. Census administration

**Description:** The objective of this project is administering the census every 5 years.

**Management**: CEOs, mathematicians, teachers and others from the world, with the help of the United Nations.

**Start day:** 1 October 2023

**Completion day:** 31 December 2023

**Budget:** $8,000,000 every 5 year

**Results after implementation:** Saving millions of unproductive hours lives, helping to improve the standards of living for all, saving over $22,000,000/year with better administration of the planet, better service for all people, etc.

**Comments:** Census is necessary to better assist the people. It is also useful for delimitations, special cards, etc. A census will take place every 5 years – starting, for example, on October 1st, 2023 - and all people will receive a special credit card (SCC), with their photo and other personal data. The delimitations between regions, and between sub-regions, will be adjusted by the census.

# Project 29. Special Credit Cards administration

**Description:** The objective of this project is to help with the administration of the special credit cards for all people.

**Management**: Leaders of banks from the world, with the help of the United Nations.

**Start day:** 1 November 2020

**Completion day:** continuous

**Budget:** $26,000,000/year

**Results after implementation:** Saving millions of hours of bureaucratic work, much better standards of living for all,
saving over $330,000,000/year with better services for people – there also be some small fees to recover the expenses.

**Comments:** It is a matter of common sense – all people need these cards for many things. The special credit card (SCC) will be used to buy everything, to identify for voting (no bureaucratic registration for voting – all people are automatically registered voters), for census, for travel, for medical assistance, etc.
        The current private credit cards will continue to work as usual.
        The changes of the delimitations between regions, and also sub-regions, will be inputted on these cards, and no other work is needed.

# Project 30. Virus control and elimination

**Description:** The objective of this project is a major medical effort for virus control and elimination.

**Management**: All major medical institutions of the world, with the help of the United Nations.

**Start day:** 1 November 2020

**Completion day:** continuous

**Budget:** $290,000,000/year

**Results after implementation:** Saving millions of lives, much better standards of living for all,
saving over $1,380,000,000/year in medical costs, lost productivity, etc.

**Comments:** It is a matter of common sense – all people want good health, peace, freedom, harmony and prosperity. People are something sacred for people. The enemies of the people on Earth are not other people, but viruses, microbes, bad bacteria and hundreds of deadly illnesses – all people on Earth will work together against these real enemies for all of us.

France, Paris: Place de la Concorde: the north side of the Egyptian obelisk (circa 1250 BC), with hieroglyphics about the pharaoh Ramses the Great (1303 BC – 1213 BC (90 years), reign 1279 BC – 1213 BC (66 years)). The obelisk is from Luxor, rises 23 m, weights 250 t and it was placed here by the King Louis Philippe I (1773 – 1850, reign 1830 – 1848) in 1836, On the pedestal are drawn diagrams showing the techniques used for transportation. The original cap was stolen in Luxor around 550 BC, and the French Government added a gold-leafed pyramid cap in 1998.

## Project 31. Non-violence implementation

**Description:** The objective of this project is simply to eliminate all forms of violence.

**Management**: All the medical institutions of the world, with the help of the United Nations.

**Start day:** 1 November 2020

**Completion day:** continuous

**Budget:** $73,000,000/year

**Results after implementation:** Saving millions of lives, much better standards of living for all,
saving over $651,000,000/year in medical costs, loss production, etc.

**Comments:** It is a matter of common sense – all people want non-violence, peace, freedom, good health, harmony and prosperity. Non-violence is directly related to medical assistance. Non-violence is a strict requirement for all activities on Earth. The first rule for everybody on Earth comes from the Hippocratic Oath: Primum non nocere - first do not harm.

# Project 32. Doctors' home visits implementation

**Description:** The objective of this project is simply to improve people's heath by having regular doctors' home visits.

**Management**: All the leaders of the medical institutions of the world, with the help of the United Nations.

**Start day:** 1 November 2020

**Completion day:** continuous

**Budget:** $931,000,000/year

**Results after implementation:** Saving millions of lives, much better standards of living for all,
saving over $7,340,000,000/year in medical expenses, loss production, etc.

**Comments:** It is a matter of common sense – all people want good health, peace, freedom, harmony and prosperity. Home visits will be a real joy! Medical doctors and assistants will make regular home visits to all people, to keep them healthy, and to prevent illnesses.

Venezia: Palazzo Flangini (right) and other palazzini on the north bank of Canal Grande, 220 m east of Ponte degli Scalzi.

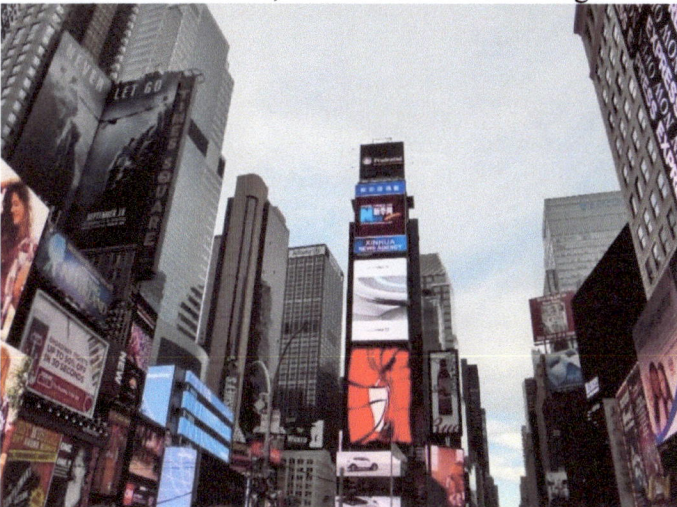

USA, New York: Times Square: 7$^{th}$ Ave (right straight), Broadway (center straight), W 43$^{rd}$ St (left and right), Marriott Marquis (right), Bertelsmann Building (left), Conde Nast Building (next), looking south.

## Project 33. Truth promotion

**Description:** The objective of this project is simply to return to the truth.

**Management**: All the leaders in the world, with the help of the people.

**Start day:** 1 November 2020

**Completion day:** continuous

**Budget:** $6,000,000/year

**Results after implementation:** Saving millions of hours lost because of lies, much better standards of living for all,
saving over $470,000,000/year with better services based on truth, increased confidence and trust, etc.

**Comments:** It is a matter of common sense – all people need the truth in order to have peace, freedom, good health, harmony and prosperity. People want truth only and collaboration. People need only truth in order to create a long term peaceful and harmonious society. If someone lies – medical treatment will follow.

Italy, Rome (753 BC), Forum Romanum, the northwest side of
Arcus Septimii Severi (left, 203, Septimius Severus (145 – 211)),
the northeast side of Templum Saturni (center, 497 BC, 42 BC, 380),
Tabularium (right up, 78 BC by Lucius Cornelius Sulla).

Switzerland, Geneva, on Pont du Mont Blanc (1862, 1965, 252 m
by 26.8 m, over Rhône River), first flag is Food and Agriculture
Organization of the United Nations, second flag is the UN flag.

## Project 34. Freedom implementation

**Description:** The objective of this project is simply to have freedom for everybody.

**Management**: All the leaders in the world, with the help of the United Nations.

**Start day:** 1 November 2020

**Completion day:** continuous

**Budget:** $370,000,000/year

**Results after implementation:** Saving millions of unproductive hours, much better standards of living for all,
saving over $2,440,000,000/year by eliminating the many errors due to not having freedom, better enjoyment of life for everybody, etc.

**Comments:** It is a matter of common sense – all people want freedom, peace, good health, harmony and prosperity. Freedom is a fundamental requirement on Earth. It is well understood that this freedom refers to doing good things in a civilized manner, not for war, violence or similar bad things, which are against the wellbeing of the people. Freedom goes hand in hand with responsibility. People can assemble peacefully only.

# Project 35. Economy improvement

**Description:** The objective of this project is simply to have a better economy for all.

**Management**: All the leaders in the world, with the help of the United Nations.

**Start day:** 1 November 2020

**Completion day:** continuous

**Budget:** $78,000,000/year

**Results after implementation:** Saving millions of unproductive hours, much better standards of living for all,
saving over $3,690,000,000/year by eliminating obsolete techniques, improving quality, etc.

**Comments:** It is a matter of common sense – all people want better economy, peace, freedom, good health, harmony and prosperity. The free market economy is not perfect, but it will be improved. All people will have the option to choose between friendly private services, and friendly government services. Independent assistants and monitors will make sure that there are no abuses. Sine qua non requirements for happiness are morality and free market.

## Project 36. Religion collaboration

**Description:** The objective of this project is to encourage collaboration between different religions, for the benefit of all people.

**Management**: Pope Francis and other religious leaders in the world, with the help of the United Nations.

**Start day:** 1 November 2020

**Completion day:** continuous

**Budget:** $40,000/year

**Results after implementation:** Saving millions of people from religious conflicts, much better standards of living for all, saving over $870,000,000/year in medical expenses, economic loss, etc.

**Comments:** It is a matter of common sense – all people want peace, freedom, good health, harmony and prosperity.

## Project 37. Government improvement

**Description:** The objective of this project is simply to make the World Government better.

**Management**: CEOs, scientists and other specialists from the world, with the help of the United Nations.

**Start day:** 1 November 2020

**Completion day:** continuous

**Budget:** $54,000,000/year

**Results after implementation:** Saving millions of unproductive hours, improving services for having much better standards of living for all,
saving over $620,000,000/year from the elimination of bureaucratic work, unnecessary formalities, etc.

**Comments:** It is a matter of common sense – all people want better government. People of course can petition the small Word Government, and can change it anytime, if it does not perform as expected.

# Project 38. Balanced budget

**Description:** The objective of this project is simply to balance the budget, like every good family does.

**Management**: Mathematicians, CEOs and other experts from the world.

**Start day:** 1 November 2020

**Completion day:** continuous

**Budget:** $68,000/year

**Results after implementation:** Saving millions of unproductive hours, improving efficiency,
saving over $370,000/year by eliminating unnecessary programs, improving quality of services for people, etc.

**Comments:** It is a matter of common sense – all people want peace, freedom, good health, harmony, prosperity and balanced budget. All budgets will have surplus of 2% - there will be a strict application of the Latin aphorism: "Sumptus censum ne superset" (Let not your spending exceed your income).

## Project 39. Errors elimination

**Description:** The objective of this project is simply to eliminate the many thousands of errors, which accumulated over the years.

**Management**: Mathematicians, CEOs, teachers and other experts from the world.

**Start day:** 1 November 2020

**Completion day:** continuous

**Budget:** $750,000/year

**Results after implementation:** Saving millions of hours wasted because of the errors, improving quality,
saving over $4,220,000/year by not having repetitive tasks due to errors, having faster services for people, etc.

**Comments:** It is a matter of common sense – all people want errors-free government, peace, freedom, good health, harmony and prosperity. It is a burning issue - correcting errors is a permanent duty for everybody - Darwin (circa 140 years ago) said "To kill an error is as good a service as, and sometimes even better than, the establishing of a new truth or fact."

## Project 40. Kindness always

**Description:** The objective of this project is simply to always have kindness for everybody.

**Management**: Teachers, doctors and volunteers from the world.

**Start day:** 1 November 2020

**Completion day:** continuous

**Budget:** $80,000/year

**Results after implementation:** Saving millions of hours lost to stress, improving the quality of life,
saving over $560,000/year by eliminating negative attitudes and conflicts, better services for people, etc.

**Comments:** It is a matter of common sense – all people want kindness, peace, freedom, good health, harmony and prosperity. Kindness is a necessity – it is a requirement for everybody. Seneca (circa 1,960 years ago) said "Wherever there is a human being, there is an opportunity for a kindness." This is a fundamental idea which must be constantly applied.

Italy, Rome (753 BC), Villa Borghese (1630), Lake Garden, from
Viale del Lago, Tempio di Esculapio (1786, Temple of Asclepius
(god of medicine, healing, rejuvenation and physicians)) on artificial
island; on front, in Greek "To Asclepius the savior".

Switzerland, Geneva, a restaurant on Avenue de la Paix, 150 m west
from the Palace of Nations and 150 m southwest from the Red Cross.

## Project 41. Government mobility

**Description:** The objective of this project is to have a very mobile government, which goes to people, not vice-versa.

**Management**: Engineers, CEOs, and other experts from the world, with the help of the United Nations.

**Start day:** 1 November 2020

**Completion day:** continuous

**Budget:** $980,000/year

**Results after implementation:** Saving millions of hours spent by people going to the government, much better standards of living for all,
saving over $5,330,000/year from unnecessary work, improving the connectivity with the people, etc.

**Comments:** The more mobility the government has, the better people will be served. All levels of government will be highly mobile - changing of the capitals for the 10 regions, and for the 100 sub-regions, etc. It is necessary to move the government close to the people, to be able to quickly solve the local problems.

Italy, Rome (753 BC), the façade (114 m by 47 m, Maderno) of Basilica Sancti Petri (1506–1626, 132 m), a mass with the Pope

Switzerland, Geneva, from Quai Gustave Ador (1845-1928, President). Jet d'Eau – a large fountain pumping water at 0.5 m$^3$/s to 140 m, lit up at night.

## Project 42. Friendly World Police

**Description:** The objective of this project is to have a very friendly world police.

**Management**: All the leaders in the world, CEOs, doctors, and other experts, with the help of the United Nations.

**Start day:** 1 November 2020

**Completion day:** continuous

**Budget:** $8,000,000/year

**Results after implementation:** Saving millions of hours of unnecessary conflicts, much better quality of life for all,
saving over $54,000,000/year by eliminating misunderstandings, bureaucratic procedures, etc.

**Comments:** It is a matter of common sense – all people want peace, freedom, good health, harmony, prosperity, and friendly police to help them when necessary. Police will help people everywhere. The United Nations will change in 2-3 years (for example, by 2024) into World Police and Assistance Organization (WPAO), to help local police in case of big natural disasters or big accidents, and will report to the top 10 Advisers. The police will be located in all capitals, and help the locals. When an emergency appears, they will quickly move to solve the emergency.

The police powers will be limited, and they will know and be friend with all the people in their jurisdiction – this is the key element of a civilized and peaceful Earth.

Police will be people's friends everywhere, and they will always help people.

Prevention of bad events is the main objective of everybody. If a bad event occurs, the police and their assistants will eliminate the consequences, reestablish the normal situation, and determine why the bad event occurred, in order to improve their activity, and prevent such bad events in the future.

In order to prevent bad things, the police, doctors and their assistants will be in permanent contact with all the people, by visiting them, phone calls, e-mails, tele-videos, and mail, to keep everybody calm and happy.

Rome: Via di San Gregorio and the Arch of Constantine (315 AD, left), and the Amphitheatrum Flavium (Colosseum, 80 AD, right).

## Project 43. Non-stop Government

**Description:** The objective of this project is to assist the government to work continuously.

**Management**: All the leaders in the world, CEOs and others, with the help of the United Nations.

**Start day:** 1 November 2020

**Completion day:** continuous

**Budget:** $950,000

**Results after implementation:** Saving millions of unproductive hours, much better standards of living for all,
saving over $3,000,000/year by eliminating redundant tasks, increasing good services for all people, etc.

**Comments:** It is only normal to have always someone in the government to help. About 66% of the Government will always be working somewhere on the Earth - if people need help, they can always call the Government. Non-stop working of all world government departments – especially medical, police, emergency, volunteers – will be carefully organized.

USA, New York: On Fifth Avenue at E 40th St, at Mid-Manhattan Library, a New York Public Library (1895, 1908, 87 branches (Carnegie libraries (Andrew Carnegie (1835-1919))), 53 millions of books and other items, the 2nd largest public library in the United States (behind the Library of Congress), and the fourth largest in the world (after British Library (170 M), Library of Congress (160 M), and Library and Archives Canada (54 M)) image archive (left), having thousands of photos, posters, illustrations, and other images.

# Project 44. Respect for privacy

**Description:** The objective of this project is simply to increase the respect for privacy.

**Management**: Teachers, CEOs and other specialists from the world.

**Start day:** 1 November 2020

**Completion day:** continuous

**Budget:** $40,000/year

**Results after implementation:** Saving millions of hours wasted on privacy, better quality of life,
saving over $500,000/year by eliminating bureaucracy related to privacy, making people more secure, etc.

**Comments:** It is clear that privacy is needed. Privacy of negotiations and discussions are necessary. In order to have serious and constructive discussions and negotiations, they must be private.

Privacy and discipline are necessary for good government work.

The results will be public and preserved, but not the private discussions.

# Project 45. Polite Government

**Description:** The objective of this project is simply to create a very polite government. Impossible? No! Inevitable? Yes!

**Management**: All the leaders in the world, CEOs, doctors, and other specialists.

**Start day:** 1 November 2020

**Completion day:** continuous

**Budget:** $57,000/year

**Results after implementation:** Saving millions of unproductive hours, much better standards of living for all,
saving over $360,000/year by eliminating unpolite and incorrect activities, creating a better working atmosphere with the public, etc.

**Comments:** It is a matter of common sense – all people want polite government, peace, freedom, good health, harmony and prosperity.

It is a strict requirement for the top management, and for all others, to be highly civilized, polite, courteous, harmonious and efficient.

Who wants to work for the world government must have good manners.

Harmony in the world starts from the harmony and good manners of the people in the world government.

Because all people on Earth want to live in harmony right now, it will be relatively easy to implement this in one good and civilized country. This may include having small, beautiful and commonly agreed fences around properties, because good fences make good neighbors, and also helps with more privacy.

Paris: L'Église de la Madeleine (Magdalenae, or L'Église Sainte-Marie-Madeleine, or La Madeleine, 1842), a Roman Catholic Church in the 8th arrondissement of Paris, by Napoleon in 1806.

USA, Newport: The east side of Bellevue Avenue, near Memorial Boulevard, looking south, with many historical shops, including International Tennis Hall of Fame and Museum, and Audrian Auto Museum.

# Project 46. Conflict resolution

**Description:** The objective of this project is to eliminate all types of conflicts on Earth.

**Management**: Doctors, CEOs, police, people assistants, and other specialists from the world, with the help of the United Nations.

**Start day:** 1 November 2020

**Completion day:** continuous

**Budget:** $84,000,000/year

**Results after implementation:** Saving many lives, much better standards of living for all,
saving over $370,000,000/year by eliminating many medical expenses, economic loses, etc.

**Comments:** It is a matter of common sense – all people want no conflicts, peace, freedom, good health, harmony and prosperity.
All conflicts must not only be quickly resolved, but they also must be transformed in friendships. This is very important for long term stability. The medical personnel and others will work diligently to make sure that disputes are resolved, and then a friendship is developed. Only in this way the situation will become stable. Conflicts will be quickly resolved, and then the corrective medical treatment will include the transformation of hostility and aggressiveness into harmony and friendship. Dispute resolution is not only Government's obligation, but it will be everybody's duty. There will be professional assistance from medical personnel, police, people assistance specialists, volunteers, religious organizations, and many others, but the bottom line is that everybody must avoid disputes.

# Project 47. Common language and alphabet

**Description:** The objective of this project is simply to establish a common language and alphabet.

**Management**: Teachers, leaders in the world, with the help of the United Nations.

**Start day:** 1 November 2020

**Completion day:** 1 November 2021

**Budget:** $680,000,000

**Results after implementation:** Saving millions of unproductive hours, much better standards of living for all,
saving over $1,570,000,000/year by eliminating errors of translation, interpretation, improving productivity, etc.

**Comments:** It is a matter of common sense – all people want to easily communicate between themselves, to have peace, freedom, good health, harmony and prosperity. As a single big, over 7.7 B, family on Earth, all people must be able to communicate easily with each other. For this reason, a common language and alphabet on Earth are needed. Because English is a de facto common language now, it will be taken as the basis of the world language, let's call it Mundo, which will be taught in all schools, and used in the world government. All the other languages will continue as secondary languages. The same is true for the Latin alphabet, which will be used everywhere, with other alphabets as secondary. The teachers will have a very significant role in implementing this project.

Rome: Trajan's column (113, center-left), Chiesa Santissimo Nome di Maria al Foro Traiano. The columns were part of Basilica Ulpia.

USA, New York: On 5th Ave (right), Broadway (next left), at E 23rd St by the Flatiron (Fuller) Building (1902, 87 m, center right triangular 22-story steel-framed tower, E 22nd St behind), Madison Square Park (left).

## Project 48. Increasing global wealth

**Description:** The objective of this project is to increase the global wealth.

**Management**: CEOs, engineers, scientists, doctors, teachers and many others from the world, with the help of the United Nations.

**Start day:** 1 November 2020

**Completion day:** continuous

**Budget:** $7,000,000/year

**Results after implementation:** Saving millions of people from poverty, much better standards of living for all,
saving over $80,000,000/year by eliminating poverty-related health issues, bureaucracy related to poverty, etc.

**Comments:** It is a matter of common sense – all people want bigger global wealth, peace, freedom, good health, harmony and prosperity. Obviously, all the global wealth will be carefully used only for peace, freedom and prosperity for all. The 2018 Global Wealth Report from Credit Suisse shows that the total global wealth has reached $317 trillions (circa $41,000/person), which is encouraging, and all this wealth must be increased and used only for peace. To increase the global wealth, everybody will be encouraged to improve everything, to create, to innovate, to research, to develop, to produce new and better products for all people, etc. It is a major responsibility of the Government to increase the global wealth, and to train those in need to have better working abilities and opportunities.

USA, Newport: Cliff Walk (1985, 5.6 km, public access walkway that borders the Atlantic shore line, looking east at the Forty Steps, and to the Easton Bay). This is at the east end of Narragansett Avenue, where there is also a parking. On this Avenue, 800 m west, there is Osgood-Pell House, 1888, (William H. Osgood (1830-1896, zinc)), from 1992 office for The Preservation Society of Newport County. Ochre Court (1892, 50 rooms) is 300 m southwest, on Webster Street.

# Project 49. Bureaucracy elimination

**Description:** The objective of this project is to eliminate bureaucracy.

**Management**: CEOs, leaders in the world, mathematicians, teachers, and many others, with the help of the United Nations.

**Start day:** 1 November 2020

**Completion day:** continuous

**Budget:** $76,000,000/year

**Results after implementation:** Saving millions of unproductive hours, much better standards of living for all,
saving over $840,000,000/year by having more efficient working techniques, using automated processes, robots, etc.

**Comments:** It is a matter of common sense – all people want no bureaucracy, peace, freedom, good health, harmony and prosperity. The goal is no bureaucracy whatsoever. In a well-organized country, with all people working together in harmony, this can be accomplished in several years.
Constant attention will be focused on avoiding duplication at all levels of the world government – there must be continuous collaboration between all levels, to prevent duplication, and to eliminate it, if it was found.
*A vice is nourished by being concealed* (from Latin: Alitur vitium vivitque tegendo

# Project 50. Corruption eradication

**Description:** The objective of this project is to eradicate corruption.

**Management**: CEOs, doctors, leaders in the world, teachers, and many others, with the help of the United Nations.

**Start day:** 1 November 2020

**Completion day:** continuous

**Budget:** $57,000,000

**Results after implementation:** Saving millions of unproductive hours, much better standards of living for all,
saving over $830,000,000/year by having correct work, increased collaboration, better efficiency, etc.

**Comments:** It is a matter of common sense – all people want no corruption, peace, freedom, good health, harmony and prosperity. Everybody will work really hard to completely eliminate corruption, organized crime and drug trafficking. Those involved in such bad activities will receive corrective medical treatment, until they become good working people.

=== here 18 Oct 2020 ==========

## Project 51. Encouraging savings

**Description:** The objective of this project is simply to encourage savings.

**Management**: CEOs, mathematicians, doctors, engineers, teachers, and many others.

**Start day:** 1 November 2020

**Completion day:** continuous

**Budget:** $3,000,000/year

**Results after implementation:** Saving millions of seniors, who don't have enough money for retirement, much better standards of living for all,
saving over $40,000,000/year by eliminating borrowing costs, bureaucracy, etc.

**Comments:** It is a matter of common sense – all people want to have good savings, peace, freedom, good health, harmony and prosperity. A world reserve system will be created.

Each government department will have some reserves for special situations (natural disasters, big accidents), and the banks will also have good financial reserves.

All people will be encouraged to save some money in banks which pay 5% interest.

# Project 52. Government efficiency

**Description:** The objective of this project is to improve government efficiency.

**Management**: CEOs, mathematicians and other specialists from the world, with the help of the United Nations.

**Start day:** 1 November 2020

**Completion day:** continuous

**Budget:** $4,000,000/year

**Results after implementation:** Eliminating millions of nonproductive hours, much better standards of living for all, saving over $50,000,000/year by concentration on efficient methods for achieving good results, reducing bureaucracy, etc.

**Comments:** It is a matter of common sense – all people want efficient government, peace, freedom, good health, harmony and prosperity.

Inspectors will help the Government with the integrity and efficiency issues – always there are ways to improve the work.

Inspectors will give advice regarding integrity and efficiency, and will take corrective actions when necessary.

# Project 53. Family assistance

**Description:** The objective of this project is simply to assist all families.

**Management**: Doctors, family assistants, teachers, and all people.

**Start day:** 1 November 2020

**Completion day:** continuous

**Budget:** $90,000,000/year

**Results after implementation:** Saving millions of children with medical conditions, much better standards of living for all,
saving over $730,000,000/year by reducing medical expenses, reducing bureaucracy, improving services, etc.

**Comments:** It is a matter of common sense – all people want healthy families with happy children, peace, freedom, good health, harmony and prosperity.

Because all families need assistance from time to time, and the big 7.7 B family on Earth contains billions of small families, all of them will have the assistance they need – this will be the result of one country well organized and managed.

# Project 54. Abuse purging

**Description:** The objective of this project is to get rid of abuses, which are quite frequent.

**Management**: CEOs, police, doctors, teachers and many others, with the help of the United Nations.

**Start day:** 1 November 2020

**Completion day:** continuous

**Budget:** $700,000,000/year

**Results after implementation:** Saving millions of people who suffered abuses, much better standards of living for all,
saving over $3,440,000,000/year by eliminating loses created by abuses, improving productivity and cooperation, etc.

**Comments:** It is a matter of common sense – all people want no abuses, peace, freedom, good health, harmony and prosperity.
It is a demanding effort, after thousands of years of all kinds of abuses, but the abuses will be gone!
Special attention will be given by Advisors to avoid abuses and wrong interpretations of the rules. All assistants (doctors, mathematicians, CEOs, engineers and teachers) will closely monitor all activities, to avoid abuses and wrong interpretations of the rules.
This requirement of not having abuses is demanding – but this is a general job, not only for Government, but for everybody, as part of the big family, we just don't need abuses.
The abuse, in some places, of confiscating the land by some government bureaucrats will be eliminated – the land belongs to the people, not the government.
The abuse, in some places, of having trains, airplanes, and others making unhealthy noises, with the government support, will be eliminated – peoples' health has always priority.

The abuse, in some places, of having to change the clocks twice a year will be eliminated – only the normal local time zones will be used.

If abuses are observed, they will be immediately reported to the Government, and corrected, in general, by the People Assistance Department, which will have personnel, including medical assistants, to analyze and promptly solve the abuses. The abusers will undergo corrective medical treatment, and will pay significant financial charges.

Italy, Rome (753 BC), Arcus Constantini (315, Constantine I (born 272, emperor 306-337)) and Amphitheatrum Flavium (right 80, started by Flavius Vespasian (born 9 AD, emperor 69-79) in 70 and completed by his son Titus Flavius Vespasianus (born 39, emperor 79-81) in 80, wrongly called Colosseum).

## Project 55. Free commerce

**Description:** The objective of this project is simply to have free commerce.

**Management**: CEOs, engineers, mathematicians and many others, with the help of the United Nations.

**Start day:** 1 November 2020

**Completion day:** continuous

**Budget:** $25,000,000/year

**Results after implementation:** Saving millions of hours wasted on blocking commerce, much better standards of living for all, saving over $680,000,000/year by eliminating barriers to commerce, improving cooperation, etc.

**Comments:** It is a matter of common sense – all people want free commerce, peace, freedom, good health, harmony and prosperity.
　　　People need intense free commerce.
　　　In one country, with one market, the commerce between the people on Earth will be free of taxes, tariffs, duties, etc. – plenty of opportunities for everybody.

# Project 56. Free and responsible speech and press

**Description:** The objective of this project is simply to make sure that there is free and responsible speech and press.

**Management**: Teachers, engineers, mathematicians and many others, with the help of the United Nations.

**Start day:** 1 November 2020

**Completion day:** continuous

**Budget:** $430,000/year

**Results after implementation:** Saving millions of hours wasted on bureaucratic procedure, much better quality of life,
saving over $8,000,000/year by eliminating obsolete techniques, improving technology, etc.

**Comments:** People need free and responsible speech and press.
It is expected not to call for war, violence, or similar destructive activities. People want peace, freedom, health, friendship and prosperity.

Italy, Gate 2 to the ruins of Pompeii (650 BC, in 79 covered by ash), with a panel entitled CARPE DIEM (enjoy the day), a Latin aphorism from a poem in the Odes (book 1, number 11) in 23 BC by the Roman poet Horace (Quintus Horatius Flaccus, born December 8, 65 BC in Venusia, Roman Republic, died November 27, 8 BC, in Rome, the capital of the Roman Empire). Important lyric poetry volumes are Odes, Satires and Ars Poetica.

# Project 57. Government integrity

**Description:** The objective of this project is simply to have government integrity.

**Management**: CEOs, leaders in the world, mathematicians, and others, with the help of the United Nations.

**Start day:** 1 November 2020

**Completion day:** continuous

**Budget:** $3,000,000/year

**Results after implementation:** Saving millions of wasted hours, much better standards of living for all,
saving over $760,000,000/year by eliminating unnecessary procedures, increasing honesty and veracity, etc.

**Comments:** It is a matter of common sense – all people want government integrity, peace, freedom, good health, harmony and prosperity.

## Project 58. Peaceful assemble

**Description:** The objective of this project is simply to have peaceful assembly.

**Management**: Teachers, police, doctors, and others.

**Start day:** 1 November 2020

**Completion day:** continuous

**Budget:** $80,000/year

**Results after implementation:** Saving millions of wasted hours, much better quality of life for all,
saving over $630,000/year by eliminating unnecessary waste of resources, improving cooperation, etc.

**Comments:** People want peaceful assembly, when needed.
If some disagree with a decision, they can always inform the government, which will respond in 3 days. The discussion will continue with calm and respect, until everything is clarified.
People can assemble peacefully only, with police for help. It is expected not to call for war, violence, or similar destructive activities. People want peace, freedom, health, friendship and prosperity. If some use violence, they will undergo corrective medical treatment, and will pay significant financial charges.

Constanta, Romania, Piazza Ovidiu: Statue of Publius Ovidius Naso (20 March 43 BC, in Sulmona – 17, in Tomis, Moesia (now Constanta, Romania), aged 60.

## Project 59. Jobs for all

**Description:** The objective of this project is simply to create jobs for all.

**Management**: CEOs, doctors, engineers, people assistants, mathematicians, teachers and others.

**Start day:** 1 November 2020

**Completion day:** continuous

**Budget:** $70,000,000/year

**Results after implementation:** Saving millions of people from poverty, much better standards of living for all,
saving over $860,000,000/year by eliminating unemployment, improving productivity, etc.

**Comments:** It is a matter of common sense – all people want jobs, peace, freedom, good health, harmony and prosperity.
       There will always be plenty of jobs at world minimum wage (assisting other people, for example), and the standard situation will be this: more jobs than available people, so people will choose the jobs they like the most.

# Project 60. Clean and safe streets

**Description:** The objective of this project is simply to have clean and safe streets everywhere.

**Management**: Police, people assistants, doctors, teachers, and many others, with the help of the United Nations.

**Start day:** 1 November 2020

**Completion day:** continuous

**Budget:** $4,000,000/year

**Results after implementation:** Saving millions of people from unhealthy streets, much better standards of living for all,
saving over $73,000,000,000/year by eliminating street infections, reducing medical expenses, improving houses, etc.

**Comments:** It is a matter of common sense – all people want clean and safe streets, peace, freedom, good health, harmony and prosperity.
People want no unemployment, no homelessness, no begging, no tipping - just all working harmoniously, having good houses, and helping each other. When necessary, corrective medical treatment and significant financial charges will be applied.

Italy, the entrance to the modern city of Pompei, located southeast of the ruins of the ancient Pompeii (650 BC, in 79 covered by ash).

USA, Newport: Cliff Walk (1985, 5.6 km, public access walkway that borders the Atlantic shore line, looking south, with the Easton Bay on the left).

# Project 61. Constitution stability

**Description:** The objective of this project is to help the Constitution stability.

**Management**: CEOs, leaders in the world, mathematicians, and others, with the help of the United Nations.

**Start day:** 1 November 2020

**Completion day:** continuous

**Budget:** $68,000

**Results after implementation:** Saving millions of wasted hours, much better standards of living for all,
saving over $354,000/year by eliminating bureaucratic procedures, increasing world stability, etc.

**Comments:** It is a matter of common sense – all people want stability, peace, freedom, good health, harmony and prosperity.
The Constitution of the World can be improved when 66% of the voters agree.

Geneva (121 BC under Romans), Avenue de la Paix 19,
International Committee of the Red Cross, founded by Jean Henri
Dunant (1828-1910) on Feb. 9, 1863, three Nobel Peace Prizes.

USA, New York: On W 42$^{nd}$ St at Avenue of the Americas, with
Bryant Park (center dawn), and Chrysler building (back center left).

# Project 62. Space exploration

**Description:** The objective of this project is simply to enhance space exploration.

**Management**: Mathematicians, engineers, and other specialists from the world, with the help of the United Nations.

**Start day:** 1 November 2021

**Completion day:** continuous

**Budget:** $600,000,000/year

**Results after implementation:** Employing millions of people, much better standards of living for all,
saving over $1,700,000,000/year by eliminating obsolete technology, improving collaboration, inventing new technology, etc.

**Comments:** It is a matter of common sense – all people want to explore the space, peace, freedom, good health, harmony and prosperity.
    The purpose for all people on Earth is to be healthy, to live in peace, freedom and harmony, to be prosperous, and to prepare to expand to the Moon, asteroids, Mars, and other places in the Universe, which can support life.

# Project 63. Robots and automated processes for people

**Description:** The objective of this project is to have many robots and automated processes for people, to live better.

**Management**: CEO and engineers from these fields.

**Start day:** 1 November 2020

**Completion day**: continuous

**Budget:** $30,000,000/

**Results after implementation:** Saving lives with medical robots, much better standards of living for all, saving over $340,000,000/year by increasing productivity, reducing bureaucracy, etc.

**Comments:** It is clear that robots and automated processes for people will help them to live better.

Important immediate objectives for everybody are to reserve time for happiness, use robots and automated processes, work less, and spend more time with your family.

Make civilized behavior and harmony everywhere an important issue.

Eliminate stress.

Help friends and colleagues.

Keep everybody relaxed, calm, friendly, patient, and happy.

# Project 64. Starting a new structure of the world

**Description:** The objective of this project is to start a new structure of the world.

**Management**: CEOs, doctors, leaders in the world, with the help of the United Nations.

**Start day:** 1 November 2020

**Completion day:** 1 January 2021

**Budget:** $700,000,000

**Results after implementation:** Saving millions of lives, much better standards of living for all,
saving over $1,920,000,000,000/year from eliminating the war budgets.

**Comments:** It is a matter of common sense – all people want peace, freedom, good health, harmony and prosperity.

To start this new structure of the world, one idea could be this: the first Honorific World Observer (from UN, for example) could invite 10 Presidents form big countries (like USA, China, Russia, UK, India, France, Japan, Germany, Brasil, and Egypt) to be the first 10 Advisors Level 4, starting, for example, on January 1st, 2021, for 10 months, until November 1st, 2021, when the new calm and noiseless elections will take place. The same for the 100 Advisers Level 3, and so on.

It is a little difficult at the beginning, but people will certainly succeed.

# Project 65. Books for helping people

**Description:** The objective of this project is simply to help people with good books

**Management**: Teachers, mathematicians, doctors, and many others.

**Start day:** 1 November 2020

**Completion day:** continuous

**Budget:** $14,000/year

**Results after implementation:** Knowledgeable people who can build a new world, much better standards of living for all, saving over $386,000/year by eliminating incorrect procedures, increasing productivity and quality, etc.

**Comments:** Good books are always useful, especially when people want to achieve peace, freedom, good health, harmony and prosperity.
　　　For better understanding and easier implementation of the World Constitution, the following books, by Michael M. Dediu, are recommended:
- Our Future is Sustainable Peace and Prosperity – Moving from conflicts to harmony and peace
– Our Future Depends on Good World Educations – Moving from frail education to solid education.
– Friendly, Helpful & Smart World Management - Moving from bureaucracy to responsive world management
– If You Want Peace, Prepare for Peace! – Moving from preparation for war to preparation for peace
– World with One Country & its Ten Friendly Regions - Moving from 195 disagreeing countries, to 1 country with 10 collaborating regions

– After 10,000 Years of Conflicts, People want 10,000 Years of Harmony - Moving from continuous wars to stable peace

- The Constitution of the World – Moving from many unsustainable constitutions, to just one Constitution of the World

- World Constitution Implementation – Moving from violent changes, to smooth transition to the Constitution of the World

- It is getting truer and truer – we urgently need the World Constitution: Moving from anarchic changes, to balanced transition to the Constitution of the World

- World Constitution with Lovely Comments - Moving from many suboptimal constitutions to the much better Constitution of the World

- World Constitution with Questions & Answers – Moving from many obsolete constitutions to the much better Constitution of the World

USA, New York: At 1501 Broadway at 43$^{rd}$ St (left), looking west, in Times Square, classic beautifully ornate Paramount Building

Italy, Rome (753 BC), Piazza del Campidoglio (1546 by
Michelangelo, paving completed in 1940, on Collis Capitolinus, the
oldest part of Rome, with Temple of Jupiter (509 BC)), a replica of
the equestrian bronze statue (175, the oldest, moved here in 1538)
of Marcus Aurelius (born 121, Emperor 161-180), Palazzo
Senatorio (right, 1350, bell-tower 1582, atop Tabularium, now the
city hall), Palazzo Nuovo (left, 1603-1654, opened 1734).

# Project 66. Hurricane prevention

**Description:** The objective of this project is to prevent hurricanes.

**Management**: Good engineers, mathematicians, CEOs, and other specialists from the world, with the help of the United Nations.

**Start day:** 1 November 2020

**Completion day:** continuous

**Budget:** $1,400,000,000/year

**Results after implementation:** Saving many lives, much better standards of living for all,
saving over $40,000,000,000/year by avoiding catastrophic losses, improving quality of life, etc.

**Comments:** Hurricanes can be prevented with some significant engineering techniques – all depends on the good management of this project.

Japan: The north side of the Osaka Castle (1597, 58 m, by Toyotomi Hideyoshi, rebuilt, with a museum), 5 km southeast of Shin-Osaka.

Italy, Rome (753 BC), on Via dei Fori Imperiali (for pedestrians only on holidays), Amphitheatrum Flavium (80, called Colosseum, back), Basilica of Maxentius and Constantine (312, right).

# Project 67. Working for long term harmony

**Description:** The objective of this project is to create conditions for long term harmony.

**Management**: CEOs, doctors, leaders in the world, with the help of the United Nations.

**Start day:** 1 November 2020

**Completion day:** continuous

**Budget:** $17,000,000/year

**Results after implementation:** Saving many lives, much better standards of living for all,
saving over $340,000,000/year by eliminating errors, improving collaboration, etc.

**Comments:** It is a matter of common sense – all people want long term harmony, peace, freedom, good health, and prosperity.
       The object is to have at least 10,000 years of harmonious living on the happy Earth.

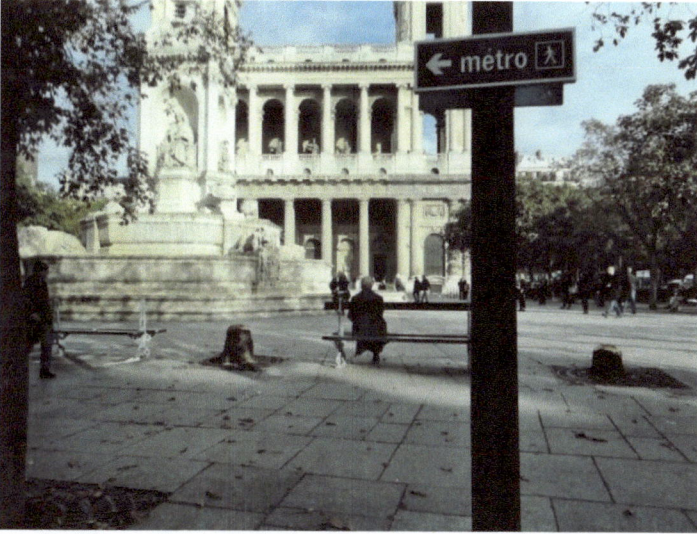

Paris: Place Saint-Sulpice, east from Rue Bonaparte, with Fontaine Saint-Sulpice and l'Église Saint-Sulpice (1646-1780, 113x58x34 m, second largest after Notre-Dame), north-west of Jardin du Luxembourg.

UK, London: the upper part of the western façade and entrance of Westminster Abbey (960, 1517, Anglican abbey with daily services, and all coronations since 1066, tower height 69 m).

# Project 68. Working for the new World Constitution

**Description:** The objective of this project is simply to promote the new World Constitution.

**Management**: Teachers, leaders in the world, with the help of the United Nations.

**Start day:** 1 November 2020

**Completion day:** continuous

**Budget:** $16,000/year

**Results after implementation:** Saving many of lives, much better standards of living for all,
saving over $320,000/year by eliminating incorrect work, improving cooperation, etc.

**Comments:** It is very clear that all people want peace, freedom, good health, harmony and prosperity.

It is nice to know that the Constitution of the World is ready to come into force, and to be put into practice, for the benefit of all people on Earth, on 6 March 2020, and it is ready to remain into force, and enjoyed by all people, at least until 6 March 12020.

# Project 69. Noise reduction and elimination

**Description:** The objective of this project is to reduce and eliminate noise by using advanced technology.

**Management**: Engineers, mathematicians, doctors, and other specialists, with the help of the United Nations.

**Start day:** 1 November 2020

**Completion day:** continuous

**Budget:** $34,000,000/year

**Results after implementation:** Saving millions of people from noise damages, much better standards of living for all,
saving over $631,000,000/year by reducing medical expenses generated by noise, improving quality of life, etc.

**Comments:** It is a matter of common sense – all people want quiet atmosphere, peace, freedom, good health, harmony and prosperity.
There are many advanced technologies, which can significantly reduce or eliminate noise everywhere – all depends on the good management of this project.

# Project 70. Zero-injury everywhere

**Description:** The objective of this project is simply to eliminate injuries everywhere.

**Management**: Doctors, engineers, mathematicians, CEOs, and other specialists, with the help of the United Nations.

**Start day:** 1 November 2020

**Completion day:** continuous

**Budget:** $360,000,000/year

**Results after implementation:** Saving many of lives, much better standards of living for all,
saving over $1,530,000,000/year by reducing medical expenses and economic losses, improving quality of life, etc.

**Comments:** It is a matter of common sense – all people want zero-injuries, peace, freedom, good health, harmony and prosperity.
    Using advanced technology, the injuries can be avoided everywhere.

## Project 71. Zero-incident everywhere

**Description:** The objective of this project is simply to eliminate incidents everywhere.

**Management**: Police, doctors, teachers, CEOs, and others, with the help of the United Nations.

**Start day:** 1 November 2020

**Completion day:** continuous

**Budget:** $340,000,000/year

**Results after implementation:** Saving many lives, much better standards of living for all,
saving over $1,710,000,000/year by reducing medical expenses, improving quality of life, etc.

**Comments:** It is a matter of common sense – all people want zero-incidents, peace, freedom, good health, harmony and prosperity.
    Using advanced technology, the incidents can be avoided everywhere.

## Project 72. Earthquake forecasting

**Description:** The objective of this project is to better forecast earthquakes.

**Management**: Good mathematicians, engineers, and other specialists, with the help of the United Nations.

**Start day:** 1 November 2020

**Completion day:** continuous

**Budget:** $400,000,000/year

**Results after implementation:** Saving millions of lives, much better standards of living for all,
saving over $60,000,000,000/year by reducing the medical expenses, buildings damages, economic losses, etc.

**Comments:** It is a difficult task, but with more concentrated technology efforts, much better forecasting can be achieved.

## Project 73. Other ideas for projects

There are many thousands for very important and urgent world projects, which will employ millions of people for very useful purposes – here are some examples:

- Flood prevention – it is possible with advanced technology.
- Drought prevention - it is possible with advanced technology.
- Dental assistance – all people will have access to good dental assistance
- Trees maintenance – all trees need maintenance, and it will be done the right way
- Sewer maintenance – all people will have public sewer and it will be properly maintained
- Product quality control – all products will be of good quality, for customers' benefit
- Home services – all home services will be easily available
- Business-customer harmony – it will be achieved
- Mortgages for people – less than 5 pages, no fees, less than 3 days

Many such projects are waiting to be implemented, for people's benefit!

France, Paris, La Seine, on Parisis boat, looking upstream to the left bank, towards east: Port de Suffren with Vedettes de Paris Croisières (Cruises), near Quai Branly, the north-west and south-west sides of la Tour Eiffel (1889, 324 m, 279 m at the 3rd level observatory), with pilier north on the left, pilier est on the center left back, pilier vest on the center front, and pilier south on the right; the south-east end of Pont d'Iéna (1808-1814, named by Napoléon after his victory in 1806 at the Battle of Jena, 1937, 155 m by 35 m, left).

www.ingramcontent.com/pod-product-compliance
Lightning Source LLC
Chambersburg PA
CBHW080048240326
41599CB00052B/33